peaceworld

peaceworld

Michael McIntyre
Sister Luke Tobin
Hazel T. Johns
Cartoons by Claudius

Friendship Press . New York

Acknowledgments

42--from Religion and Violence by Robert McAfee Brown. Copyright © 1973, Robert McAfee Brown. Used by permission of Westminster Press.

56--from the Robert McNamara speech "The Goals of the Second Development Decade." By permission of Catholic Mind.

56, 63-67--from Faith and Violence by Thomas Merton. Reprinted with permission from the University of Notre Dame Press, Notre Dame, Indiana 46556.

69-70--from Social Justice and the Latin Churches: Proceedings, Conference on Church and Society in Latin America, translated by Jorge Lara-Braud. © 1969. By permission of John Knox Press.

70--from My Life for My Friends: The Guerilla Journal of Nestor Paz, by Nestor Paz, translated by Ed Garcia and John Eagelson. © 1975. Used by permission of Orbis Books.

72-73--from Value Clarification as Learning Process: A Handbook for Christian Educators, by Brian Hall and Maury Smith. © 1974. Used by permission of Paulist-Newman Press.

Art Credits

14, 75-77, 103, 111--IDAC Document 7, Claudius

80, 93, 96--IDAC Document 2, Claudius

Library of Congress Cataloging in Publication Data

Johns, Hazel T   1920-
  Peaceworld.

        Includes bibliographical references.
        1. Peace (Theology) 2. Violence--Moral and
religious aspects. 3. Nonviolence--Moral and religious
aspects. 4. Peace. I. McIntyre, Michael, 1942-
joint author. II. Tobin, Luke, 1908-   joint author.
III. Title.
BT736.4.J63   261.8   76-12410
ISBN 0-377-00054-X

Contents

Preface

Behind *Peaceworld* there is a bit of history. Under the umbrella of the National Council of Churches there is a great deal of interdenominational activity—including the formation of task forces designed to carry out specific assignments. We who came together as a task force on "The Mission of Building Peace" committed ourselves to the best means possible to undergird the efforts of Christians in all walks of life toward the goal of true peace.

We shared a common concern but represented a variety of denominational heritages and even a differing language vocabulary. Some members of the group were members of historic "peace" churches, while others were members of churches which traditionally have not given major focus to this specific issue. In the attempt to find a common denominator with which to begin our work the following definition of peace evolved through a group process involving nearly thirty people. It is not perfect—it is the creation of human beings, reflecting the individual and corporate anxiety, frustration and hopeful yearning for a peaceful world felt by us all.

"Peace is a world in which neither the overt violence of war nor the covert violence of unjust systems is used as an instrument for extending the interests of a particular nation or group. It is a world where basic human needs are met, and in which justice can be obtained and conflict resolved through nonviolent processes and human and material resources are shared for the benefit of all people."

Our authors were asked to claim what they found valid in the definition and apply it in the pursuit of their particular focus, namely: (1) a biblical-theological background for understanding peace; (2) an examination of personal and social values to determine the extent to which violence permeates our society; and (3) case studies centering around the relationships among the issues of hunger, population and resources as related to peace.

The result, *Peaceworld*, embodies a great and imaginative dream. It is central to our Christian faith, not as we have so often processed it, but as we now increasingly know it must be realized to fulfill God's purposes for his children. Our guest, Bishop Abel T. Muzorewa, our authors, Michael McIntyre, Sister Luke Tobin, Hazel Johns and cartoonist, Claudius Ceccon, have each contributed unique but integrating content which instructs us in the ways of Christ toward a "peaceworld."

Behind *Peaceworld* there is history, yes. Before us is hope, and a dream, and the ways of obedience to Him who is the Prince of the "peaceworld" coming to be.

Bruce L. Jones, Chairperson
Task force on "The Mission of
Building Peace"

Introduction————

"Peaceworld" is a world we all are seeking. It is not the world of free spirits in the millenium, but rather a world of flesh, bones, and blood to be enjoyed now by all the people of the earth. This is the kind of world the authors of this book are projecting.

In Scripture, Reverend McIntyre finds the basis for such a world —a world in which those with abundance share with those in need, a world in which social injustices are eliminated or are reduced to a minimum, a world in which love is preached and practiced in brotherhood. Unfortunately, we are still living in a world of greed and selfishness. Take, for instance, my country of Rhodesia. The white settlers who number only five percent of the population have been given one-half the land, and the best land at that. Laws have been enacted to protect the rich and powerful at the expense of the poor and deprived blacks. Salaries of whites average about ten times those paid to blacks. Education is practically free for white children while black parents have to build schools and pay fees for their children. The whole pattern of society is unjust and it is for a change in these structures that Rhodesia must struggle. So far our struggle has been largely nonviolent, but our patience is running out and if there are not some basic changes in the whole social pattern, violence will erupt from the Zambeze to the Limpopo. All these realities force us to search Scripture, not seeking false comfort, for we know that Scripture is more like dynamite than talcum powder! But we need to know that our friends in the United States and Canada wrestle with Scripture, too.

Sister Luke Tobin speaks about systematic changes which must occur, that is, basic changes in the structure of society. Church people in Rhodesia are deeply involved in trying to make these changes · peaceful. I, as a church leader, feel called to stand up for my people to help eliminate the injustices of the current way of life in my country.

To my North American friends I ask, "What are you doing?" As we see it from afar there are many injustices in your own society.

The gap between the rich and poor is ever widening in North America. Racial and social discrimination are still practiced as seen in the Boston and Louisville school busing incidents which the rest of the world watched.

A few years ago I saw and keenly felt such discrimination when I was studying in the United States. I cannot easily forget how it hurt me and many of my fellows. As Hazel T. Johns enumerates in Part Three, we saw you use your economic and military force to get your way in the world. It was the way of the bully and the overlord. Your great consumption of scarce world resources needed for the developing nations is considered unfair and anti-social by many of us. In fact, Americans are to the world what whites are to Rhodesia: selfish, greedy, affluent and inconsiderate. You do not want to be these things, but you are in so many instances.

Take, for instance, the issue of chrome. When Ian Smith declared the independence of Rhodesia without considering the wishes of the ninety-five percent black population, the United Nations formally voted to boycott Rhodesian products. Later through the Byrd Amendment, the U.S. broke the sanctions agreement for which it had voted. This did two things: (1) it put the U.S. in a bad light—as irresponsible and selfish in the eyes of other nations; and (2) it gave more economic strength to a repressive government in Rhodesia. The same bad image was created in Africa by U.S. support of the dictatorial Salazar regime in Portugal during the years the former Portuguese colonies in Africa and Asia were struggling for independence.

Peaceworld will be a futile book and will not truly speak to the needs of the human family if it does not lead you to look at the kinds of situations in the world, political and economic in nature, which make and keep human life unjust and unfair.

But just as I have known that Americans have done these things to the rest of the world through governmental policy, I also know that many men and women of good will want to have a new day. They want an alternative vision and reality for a new humanity. To all who will listen and hear, look and see, I commend this book with the hope that "peaceworld" may be born of our struggling.

Bishop Abel T. Muzorewa

Part One

The Biblical / Theological Background for Peace

Michael McIntyre

1. The Lift of a Driving Dream

Those who repent and join God's struggle for justice are given a promise: we are going to win. The Good News of the Old and New Testaments is simply that. God and all the people belonging to God are going to prevail over the darkness. There are and there will be setbacks in history. Humanity will continue to be inhumane at times; selfishness will continue to embarrass us; greed will make us narrow and grasping; infidelities will shame us; hatreds will continue to make us bitter. But not one of these human downfallings will overcome the reality of the triumph of God's work in human history. In spite of us and with us, God's word of justice, liberty, freedom and hope will continue to be proclaimed and heard. Just when we think that it is going to be lost, it will spring forth anew. The powers of darkness will not be able to overcome it. God's word will not return empty. The meaning of all this is beautiful and persistent: the cause we represent as God's people is fated to prevail. This promise has remained true with stunning, stubborn accuracy through the ages. It is not a false promise. Each age must wrestle with the meaning of the promise in its own social context. Like bread, the promise has the power to nourish and sustain the life of God's people.

Sometimes a few selected words come to symbolize the power of the promise. For those before us, liberty, equality and fraternity served to carry hopes and dreams. In our moment, the words of justice, liberation, self-development and human fulfillment serve for many as the symbolic words of promise which can give what former President Nixon liked to call "the lift of a driving dream." Yet, not everyone feels comfortable with these words. For some these words convey unrest, turbulence, uncertainty and chaos. Such fears make some of us unable to participate in the words of promise which have come into the midst of our time as compelling images. Still, whether or not we are able to participate, the mounting hope in the world for justice, liberation, self-development and human fulfillment amounts to a flood tide in our history. Part of the purpose of this book is to make these words understandable, to give them meaning beyond fear and frustration.

The mission of building peace in our era is directly related to the way we capture the sweeping historical reality implied in the promise of these words and align ourselves and our institutions with them. If we give these visions a body, a substance, a texture and a positive meaning in our own setting, we will have come a long way toward understanding the mission of building peace.

Experiencing Unfairness

Begin this task by observing that one of the common human experiences in all places and times is the experience of unfairness. All of us know something about this. All of us have witnessed or experienced economic unfairness, political unfairness and social unfairness. When we speak of the great hopes for justice, liberation, self-development and human fulfillment we are also saying that we hope for the reduction of unfairness in life. If troubled by the language of justice, let us see it as the language of establishing fairness in the relationships of the whole human family. If troubled by the words of liberation, let us remember that we bring liberation to reality by working for fairness in human rights. If uneasy with the promises of self-development and human fulfillment, then let us call them the promises of fairness for each human being to be the full creation which God promised us in the person of Jesus Christ.

This biblical study of the foundations of peace assumes that the Good News is a "word" that is biased: it is biased against unfairness among humans and it is biased toward justice, liberation, self-development and human fulfillment as the forms which a concern for fairness takes in our time. Implied in this assumption is that political concerns will have to be a part of any faithful study of the biblical passages we examine. To say that the study of the Bible involves political realities is not to imply that the Bible takes up a partisan kind of politics. That has been a misunderstanding of many people. We are not arguing for or against partisan politics. But we are suggesting that our study of the Bible has clear-cut implications for the political order. And we will make those connections. And through this study we will keep believing that God's word is not helpless in time. We are going to win. The cause we represent as God's people will prevail.

13

The biblical texts to be examined are related to the task force's working definition of peace quoted in the preface. We will pull apart this definition into sections and each biblical passage lifted up for study will help provide a basis for examining the definition.

It is important to note that this section of the book is not a biblical study in the traditional sense. Rather, it is an attempt to comment on biblical passages which may loom large in the thinking of many who must enact their discipleship in the midst of injustice and unfairness.

This approach to biblical reflection, moreover, assumes that there are a number of preconditions which have to be met before we can hope for a "peaceworld." Here we will not take it for granted that the conventional definitions of peace, either as the absence of war or as economic strength, military security and the moral use of power, have much to say to us as we seek a new way in a terribly complex world.

If some of these ways of approaching the Bible seem strange, don't puff and don't gag. Read them through and you'll find, I hope, bread, not stones.

2. Responding to Systems

"PEACE IS A WORLD IN WHICH NEITHER THE OVERT VIOLENCE OF WAR NOR THE COVERT VIOLENCE OF UNJUST SYSTEMS" is used against people. This opening affirmation included in the definition of peace makes us look at two kinds of violence. We are familiar with the violence of war; no one needs to be reminded of its pain, suffering and tragedy. But we are not so well acquainted with the hidden, or covert, violence of unjust systems. Often the accusation that hidden violence is accomplished by the way in which goods and services are produced, how and to whom they are made available and how they are bought and sold seems too complicated. Or the charge that laws are used to benefit the powerful rather then those too powerless to gain control of their own lives seems a reckless and provocative statement. Whether or not we can readily visualize these forms of hidden violence, they are likely to continue. The call to church people and to all of God's people is for us to try to understand these connections and to respond at the starting point of justice—not charity or generosity alone.

To this point our biblical viewpoint offers some clues about overt and covert violence. While it is possible to find several passages in the Old Testament which make a case for "holy war" and for Israel's victories over the tribes that were being displaced by Israel's presence, the New Testament begins at another point. The word from Jesus that peacemakers are to be blessed and that enemies should be loved and forgiven seems to stand boldly in front of the war mentality of an eye for an eye and a tooth for a tooth. A new commandment to go beyond the law of tit for tat and to seek peace takes its place as an announcement of what the Kingdom of God is like. When the reign of God is firmly fixed in human affairs, war will not continue. Jesus points people to this greater hope.

In our time, this hope for peace is forced to take its place alongside the reality that those who have been the victims of covert, or hidden, violence by the powerful with their economic, legal and social systems may choose overt violence as the only adequate tool for restoring some kind of balance and justice. As Christians and as the people of God, we can hope for nonviolence to be at the heart of what is done by those who must resist the hidden forms of injustice which come to them. We ought to expect, however, that those who are driven to the breaking point by unyielding unfairness may, indeed, choose to use violence as their last resort. Thus, if we would wish to act on the basis of our hope for nonviolence, we must be sure we can see the hidden actions manipulating law, economics and politics against those who are marginal. It is to this point of unmasking unfairness that the Bible begins to speak more plainly. I Kings 21 is a good focal point to show how the Bible speaks to covert violence.

Naboth's Vineyard

To illustrate this point, look at the story of Naboth's vineyard. Briefly, the property rights of the peasant Naboth are plainly violated by King Ahab and his wife, Jezebel. Ahab desires property which has rightfully passed through generations into the holdings of Naboth. When Naboth refuses to give up what is rightfully his, Ahab and Jezebel scheme to come up with a violation of the prevailing law with which to accuse Naboth. They proclaim a fast, and Naboth is given a seat of honor. During the fast two agents of the king swear that they have heard Naboth cursing God and the king. Consequently, Naboth, without any right of appeal, is stoned to death. Ahab now legally proceeds to take possession of the vineyard. He gets away with this maneuver only to be confronted with the truth by Elijah the Tishbite. Elijah pronounces a curse on Ahab and Jezebel, prompting repentance from Ahab. Because of the king's apparent remorse, a second word from the Lord is given to Elijah, who promises that destruction will be visited not on Ahab, but on a later generation of his house.

This story establishes the power and identity of Elijah, while showing that hidden manipulation of the legal system can yield benefits to whoever is in power. But the story raises a problem that is not well answered: does any restoration of justice really arise? Is Naboth's life really paid for? Does the advantage of the stronger really change? What is to keep Ahab from acting this way again? Is the role of the prophet that of a referee who calls a foul—and then watches the game go on?

The story of Ahab and Naboth just doesn't delve into these subtleties. We cannot tell from it whether the repentance was genuine or whether it was a facade, though the delayed destruction promised by God would be one suggestion that Ahab's contrition was credible. Nor can we tell from the text whether the land in question reverted to Naboth's next of kin. The story raises as many questions as it answers. So perhaps we should turn to the New Testament account of the tax collector, Zaccheus (Luke 19:1 - 10).

The Response of Zaccheus

Jesus visits a tax collector who has spawned wealth through the manipulation of the tax system. When Jesus honors him with a visit, Zaccheus voluntarily offers to give half his possessions to charity and to repay those whom he has cheated four times over. Here, repentance is tied to action. Forgiveness and acceptance result in changed behavior. The changed behavior is directly connected to the use of a system—the taxation system—by Zaccheus. Covert violence inflicted upon people who have been cheated does not have to be met with further violence. Injustice and unfairness are set right by the decision to change what was wrong. More important, these changes spring from the heart of Zaccheus.

Not all who manipulate the systems of our society will be so willing to change and to make reparation. There are those who will deny, even while engaging in the violence of covert systems, that they are doing anything outside what is minimally permissible under existing regulations. And often, they are not. But we are called as the people of God to seek more than the minimal forms of justice. We are called to seek the restoration of things fourfold for those who have been the victims of unjust systems. And in the process we should help create an opportunity for those like Zaccheus to find their own salvation—those who use the covert violence of the unjust systems to their advantage need a word of new life and hope. Or, as Jesus says of Zaccheus, ". . . for this man too is a son of Abraham, and the Son of Man has come to seek and save what is lost."

But we also need to remember that victims of systems do not always remain victims. Sometimes they find ways to compromise themselves so thoroughly that they no longer suffer from the system—at least, not outwardly. They adjust so well to the prevailing system that they become like it, or, as educator Paulo Freire has shown us, the oppressed become like the oppressor because they have no other model. Biblical studies do not usually examine this aspect of how the insiders and the outsiders relate to each other.

Esther Caught Between

There is one book, however, which picks up this theme and explores it. While we do not do much with the book of Esther in white, middle-class American theology, people from the Pacific basin, for example, find it most instructive. Dr. Roy I. Sano, addressing the December, 1974 National Inter-Ethnic Convocation sponsored by the United Methodist Church in San Antonio, Texas, speaks to this theme:

. . .You recall Esther. Talk about making it in an alien society, she was chosen by the King. She bacame the Queen. She made it there by denying her Jewishness during a "beauty contest." Her uncle advised her to do so (Esther 2:10, 20). But after she was accepted into the inner circles she discovered she had joined a society where people with power promulgated a decree to exterminate her people. Mordecai, her uncle, reminded her of the realities of the situation. "Think not that in the King's palace you will escape any more than all other Jews. . .who knows whether you have not come to the kingdom for such a time as this" (Esther 4:13-14).

As a person who had obtained entrance into an alien society, it was time for her to assert her ethnicity and reverse the decree. At the risk of her own life, she broke the law and resisted the King's decree which was designed to exterminate the "unassimilable" Jews. Dr. Sano points out that "by some standards, we have become Esthers (Asian-Americans) to secure our acceptability, and like Esther, have denied our ethnicity in order to do so."

What Dr. Sano is doing in this passage from Esther and in his whole text is to point us face to face with the reality of those who do not choose to respond to covert violence with their own violence, but rather suffer the even deeper violence of losing their identity in the midst of the overwhelming power of those in control. We need to understand the several forms of violence and we need to see with compassion the aberrations which are caused in those who cannot find an end to the violence which is played on them by the powerful. We need to understand more fully than we have the terrible distortions of humanity which plague the powerful who must struggle to keep the upper hand. Overt and covert violence both produce "no win" situations for the victims and those who make them so. We must be clearer than we have been about these interactions. Where we automatically lined up on the side of power and privilege, we must learn to see that biblical faith dares us to hope for salvation of all, particularly those trapped in the perpetuation of violent systems.

3. The Age of the Hustle

"Peace is a world in which neither. . .overt violence. . .nor. . . covert violence. . .IS USED FOR EXTENDING THE INTERESTS OF A PARTICULAR GROUP OR NATION." In this chapter we will look at some of the ways in which particular nations and groups justify putting their interests ahead of those of the rest of the human family. This kind of unfairness in human relationships retards the self-development and human fulfillment of the world's family. It is understandable why some nations and groups work for their own self-interests. But it is not so understandable why the advantages of the stronger nations must be protected most often by the use of force and by the constant accumulation of power. To be on "top of the heap" requires enormous effort and the diversion of other energies into this one task.

Trying to Pin Jesus Down

While the Bible does not directly speak to this problem, it does lay down some important insights about the pursuit of authority, security and power and what having these "gods" can do to one. We see this in Luke 4:1-13, the story of Jesus' temptation.

Full of the Holy Spirit, Jesus returned from the Jordan, and for forty days was led by the Spirit up and down the wilderness and tempted by the devil.

All that time he had nothing to eat, and at the end of it he was famished. The devil said to him, 'If you are the Son of God, tell this stone to become bread. Jesus answered, 'Scripture says, "Man cannot live by bread alone." ' Next the devil led him up and showed him in a flash all the kingdoms of the world. 'All this dominion will I give to you,' he said, 'and the glory that goes with it; for it has been put in my hands and I can give it to anyone I choose. You have only to do homage to me and it shall all be yours.' Jesus answered him, 'Scripture says, "You shall do homage to the Lord your God and worship him alone." '

The devil took him to Jerusalem and set him on the parapet of the temple. 'If you are the Son of God,' he said, 'throw yourself down; for Scripture says, "He will give his angels orders to take care of you," and again, "They will support you in their arms for fear you should

21

strike your foot against a stone." ' Jesus answered him, 'It has been said, "You are not to put the Lord your God to the test." '

So having come to the end of all his temptations, the devil departed, biding his time.

The temptations passage is a tale about the beginning of Jesus' ministry, but it is also the tale of temptations placed before the human community. Here are promises that one's own interests can be made foremost, without consequences. Luke's version of the story adds one explanation that Matthew's version doesn't really amplify. It hints that the devil was content to bide time and wait for another chance. In fact, a textual footnote points to the devil's talk with Judas as the time when the devil acted again. In effect, the story suggests that either Jesus should have conformed to the temptations or that he should have been prepared to suffer later the hidden consequences.

The temptations held out before Jesus were all political in nature, promising him the political tools of authority and control, of security and well-being, and of power and wealth. These were tantalizing promises then, as they are now. If Jesus had changed the stones into bread, his authority and control would have been established. But he did not fall for this. Instead, in his ministry, he repeatedly chose to stand by innocence and silence, rather than authority and control. If he had leapt from the pinnacle and been saved, his security and prestige would have been assured. Instead, he chose throughout his ministry to risk vulnerability. Finally, if he had accepted the kingdoms which the devil offered, he could have established his power and wealth. But, he chose powerlessness as his way of being in the powerful world because he knew then and knows now the weakness of power and the power of weakness. With all of these rejections, the devil, like "The Godfather," Part I, set the contract on his life in motion. The word was whispered to Judas.

Trying to Pin Us Down

We are still caught in this reality and it is a truth about life which must be thought about as we look at the mission of building peace. The reality is that in every age, temptations will be made to vanity and pride, to the deep longing for authority and control, to the

22

hunger for security and well-being and to the search for personal power. All of us will be made offers we seemingly can't refuse and we can expect to be regarded every bit as passive and out of step as Jesus if we say no. For it is part of the nature of our time that we expect our system, just as others in the other developed nations expect theirs, to deliver these political advantages to us intact, on a regular basis. The advertising to which we are constantly exposed carries this message.

In fact, the competition to be the "best" society in fulfilling these expectations has propelled us into what might be called the Age of the Hustle. To "hustle" is to offer goods and gimmicks whether or not they are needed, while convincing the customer that they are necessary or important. Those who "hustle" in the name of power and prestige, authority and control, and security and well-being seem to come up as the rewarded winners time after time. But the demands generated and the deals made in the name of providing security, authority and power inevitably take their toll somewhere in the whole human family. Perhaps Jesus resisted the temptations because he knew this. Perhaps he knew that the personal search for security, authority, and power, when pursued outside of a commitment to seek a future with and for others, was a formula destined to turn one in on oneself in such an unhealthy and defensive way that community wouldn't be possible. In the face of this, his choices of silence, weakness and innocence are preferable to a false promise of personal power.

North America has witnessed several years of false promises in its political order characteristic of the "hustle." In the U.S., for example, "peace with honor" and "a full generation of peace" as measured against the political realities following their announcement, have engendered only the chaos of distrust. They were only tantalizing promises of security, authority and power. That we wanted so much to believe them only underscores the need we have to be those who possess security and well-being. In and of themselves, such deep longings are not to be condemned. But if we attempt to pursue them alone, or ask our political leadership to pursue them alone for us, apart from the common search with the human family for these gifts, we will probably end up defensive about our imagined advantage. We are at a major political watershed as we seek to choose political leadership capable of seeing itself as connected to the human family and not just to the interests of a particular group or nation.

As North America evaluates its own national purpose with the corporate history of the world, it must recognize that either it will go into the final quarter of this century able to work cooperatively with the world in the search for justice as fairness and human fulfillment or it will tighten up even tighter on the doctrine that power and wealth, security and authority, and well-being are the only fitting searches, fearful it will become a "pitiful, helpless giant." Now is the time for those who can read between the lines of the temptation story in Luke to realize that the latter approach is a false political promise engendering only chaos. Simply put, it won't work.

We are now left with one choice—the "real, human agenda." At present, it is not the preservation of U.S. security, power and authority at the expense of the rest of the world; nor is it the establishment of the security, authority and power of the Union of Soviet Socialist Republics; nor is it even the guaranteeing of the security, authority and power of all the developed nations as over against the rest of the world. The real, human agenda lies in working out with the pulsing, suffering human family the common hope for our common future. The "hustle" of North America, the U.S.S.R., and the other developed nations that somehow only their future security, authority and power matter must be named exactly for the false political words that they are.

"We Who Bear the Human Name"

But rather than labor from the view of the powerful, listen to those who must live their lives out in silence, in innocence of the great power games and even in suffering. This poem grew out of a meeting of some Asian leaders of the Christian church:

> We who bear the human name, are like flowers of the field;
> without status, without fame,
> trampled down and made to yield,
> unprotected and exposed to the scorching wind that blows.
> Let all the world now blossom as a field.

Even Solomon of old, (said our Lord, the man of peace)
with his glory and his gold could not match the flowers' grace.
We are weak, but we recall how the mighty ones must fall.
We are people of the field,
crowding Asia's city streets;
we are people called to build a community of peace.
And we remember as we toil that hope is springing from the soil.

Do you see this fragile hope springing up like grass in the middle of a concrete slab? All over Asia, Africa and Latin America millions are made to endure, like Faulkner's character, Dilsey, in *The Sound and the Fury*, through the irrational nightmares of those gone nearly mad in their search for personal security, authority and power —particularly the power of wealth. Both their own leaders and the leaders of the developed nations hold out false political promises to them which continue their own captivity to several forms of unfairness. They cry out to us for solidarity with them on the real, human agenda. They cry out to us to join them in standing for all human rights rather than for the rights of those who hustle them with false promises: the essential right to life, the right to enjoy and maintain cultural identity, the right to participate in decision-making within the community, the right to dissent, the right to personal dignity, including protection from torture, and the right to religious liberty. They wait in their silence, their humiliation, their vulnerability and their weakness, and they are like the Jesus we know who would not be tantalized. They wait with patience, hope and incredible endurance for the time when the green shoot of fairness will break through the hardpan of our hustles. They toss out this message and this hope like a clue that some of us recognize and some never do.

As we look at the way in which the interests of particular nations and groups frequently are extended in favor of the interests of all, we can see that one of the elements in the mission of building peace is for us to be clear about false promises of political power and not to be confused by anything less than the real, human agenda which stands beyond our personal advantage and which stands within God's promise that the weak will not be sent, empty, away.

4. Do More Than The Least

"PEACE IS A WORLD. . . WHERE BASIC HUMAN NEEDS ARE MET AND HUMAN AND MATERIAL RESOURCES ARE SHARED FOR THE BENEFIT OF ALL. . . ." When talking about the distribution of resources in the human family, the temptation is to believe that the question of efficiency of present systems is the only problem. Or, we end up talking about waste, ecology and budget priorities. Not one of these factors is inappropriate. But, as Christian people and as people of God we need to be sure that we are taking the concern an additional step: we need to discuss the will to share at more than minimal levels. The problem in creating the political will to go the second mile in the sharing of human and material resources is basically a theological issue. The decision to go beyond the minimal requirements for human well-being is not made easily because it requires those who have more to change their patterns of getting, having and using. The decision to move toward voluntary austerity to provide others with at least adequate amounts is a frightening and threatening reality. Voluntary austerity is an idea that for many Americans recalls the Depression and Dustbowl days and real privation. They do not take easily, therefore, to the notions of those who did not share that terrible firsthand experience but who call for significant changes.

But perhaps quality, not quantity, in the sharing and use of resources joins with the question of availability. Or, simply asked, do we need more to be more? Those who fear the specter of voluntary austerity can at least join those who welcome a less elaborate life-pattern at the point of seeking quality in life. The question "do we need more to be more?" can be the starting point for a discussion of the way the world shares its human and material resources.

David, Nabal and Abigail

There is an interesting Old Testament story which wrestles with the call to enhance our lives by going beyond the minimum of justice and sharing our human and material resources. Found in I Samuel 25, the story revolves around three main characters, David, Nabal and Abigail, during a period when King Saul and his adversary David experienced running encounters. At this point in the story we find David exiled in the wildernesses of Engedi and Paran. David's band has joined with bands of wilderness dwellers, or, more bluntly, gangs possibly ranging from quite dangerous to peaceful. David's gang, basically lawful, offers protection, with the expectation of a reward, to Nabal's shepherds tending a flock of 3,000 sheep and 1,000 goats. The season of sheepshearing has arrived and, following local custom, the owner of the flock is expected to share some of the wealth by making gifts of food available to the needy. David understands this custom and dispatches ten of his men to Nabal's home to make a claim on the gifts. Nabal responds abruptly to the request, saying he isn't going to give his goods away to just anyone. This word is brought back to David who, angered at being so callously treated, instantly starts out with 400 of his followers, leaving 200 back with the baggage, to take what is theirs.

Fortunately, Nabal's wife, Abigail, hears of the situation and acts to right the matter. She hastily gathers 200 loaves, two skins of wine, five sheep already dressed, five measures of parched grain, 100 bunches of raisins and 200 cakes of dried figs and sets out to intercept David and his followers. As they approach each other, David is highly angered and swears to kill the household. Abigail comes to him, prostrates herself and apologizes for her foolish husband. Moreover, she reminds David that he, the next likely candidate for king, must not be found with bloodguilt on him. David hears this argument and spares the household.

But the story is not finished. When Abigail returns home she finds the customary feast in progress and Nabal very drunk. Wisely, she says nothing until the morning when Nabal is again sober. Upon hearing what has happened, he is stricken with a seizure and, in a few days, he dies. Then, with what must have been great delight, the writer of I Samuel finishes the story by reporting that David takes the widow Abigail to be his wife.

The story is meant to show the evidences of God's providential protection of David and to establish even further the legitimacy of David's ascension to the throne. But it makes another point beyond this historical purpose. It also shows the sensitivity of a woman who

27

can move beyond the minimal claims of justice and make real restitution for wrongs that have been done. She recognizes the fairness of the claim made on Nabal but, unlike Nabal, she prefers to honor the claim. Not only does she provide an abundant gift of food as is proper at the time of sheepshearing, she also takes the trouble to interpret the situation. She apologizes for and corrects her husband's insensitivity, volunteers to take the blame for the incident and helps David do some face-saving by pointing out the larger meaning of David's act. She does what is minimally required and then goes several steps beyond.

Seeing It As It Is

It is toward this example we turn to consider some of the claims being made today on those of us with goods and a place in society. The question for us is whether we can, with Abigail, sense what is required beyond the minimums to give humanity and dignity to the furious, but real, claims made by the victims of unfairness. Look at some of the present-day events where the same kinds of claims and actions play themselves out and ask, "When should we be like Abigail?"

To answer, we need to see how well we can learn to distinguish fairness from unfairness. Our eyes often are blinded and our ears do not hear much of what goes on around us. We end up tolerating awful arrangements and situations because we cannot comprehend the extent of unfairness. Or, even worse, we cannot accept the fact that those in power often maintain that position by settling to their advantage and against the advantage of others. Repeatedly, Americans register shock and concern when given more details than those "officially" presented on given instances of unfairness. Instead of resulting in outrage, however, such revelations usually produce bewilderment, even cynicism. "How can we believe anybody?" is the recurring reaction. Instead of asking what requires a response like Abigail's —that is, a response which goes beyond the minimums of justice—maybe we need to raise the prior question, "What is true about a situation?"

If we are willing to question the accuracy and truth of the information in our possession, then we may well be on our way to a major building block in the mission of building peace: the willingness to question all data. A corollary of this is that we need to ask for more data from more diverse sources and that all data be viewed without apology from our biblical bias toward fairness and justice for people. It is no disservice to our own people, class or nation to seek the widest possible amount of information about given situations. Only when we have more information than the accepted ideas of our culture can we expect to be able to play the Abigail-role of making restitution, of taking blame where in error and of creating some gracious face-saving alternatives to let everyone proceed to a new beginning. Another name for this process is reconciliation. More than an abstract notion, it requires looking at Abigail's acts as possible models for our own behavior. The Bible is quite clear in saying that we have been "enlisted and entrusted" with the message of reconciliation (II Corinthians 5:18-19). Reconciliation on the basis of an honest assessment of a situation is the tough, but rewarding, ministry to which all of us in the mission of building peace are called.

There are two additional guidelines to help us in seeing unfairness and acting for fairness. Knowing where to look and knowing how to see is the first step.· The Bible suggests that our mission is to "heal the sick, raise the dead, cleanse lepers, and cast out devils. . ." (Matthew 10:8). The same passage loosely translated from the Greek text, can be altered to say, "provide therapy to those without health, lift up those without life, give acceptance to those who are outcast, and throw out that which is demonic." If we accept this call to mission, perhaps we can undertake a search for fairness and justice that will result a therapeutic, life-giving and inclusive ministry. We are not unbiblical when we admit that being peacemakers requires us to plunge into the search for fairness and justice and to act with conviction and compassion and to see the whole situation.

Secondly, in a generation in which language itself has come close to George Orwell's *1984* fantasy that "black is white" and "peace is war" we need to see if we can describe things as they really are. An "incursion" is an invasion. "Protective reaction" is bombing. "Body counts" represent dead persons. The political rhetoric which pours out on us constantly needs to be looked at, named for what it is, and moved beyond. We can do that. If we know that if something "looks like a duck, waddles like a duck and quacks like a duck, that it probably is a duck," then we will move toward helping our self-confidence in describing the life situation. When we see pictures of the

bloated bellies of babies in Bangladesh, we can observe that some systems are wrong and that it doesn't have to be this way. Move beyond the language of "Oh, those poor things. Where do we send some money?" and further observe that the systems of this world so badly askew bring their worst punishment on the children of this world. Our world fairly cries out for honest appraisals of what is going on.

We don't have to hold a Ph.D. to comment on it; we can be disciplined amateurs who cut through the flimflam of polluted language and public relations jargon to get at the central questions. It is quite important for the church to have the mission and the courage of that mission to keep in there asking the central, obvious, unresolved and painful questions which even disciplined amateurs can name. If we never move beyond this part of our mission, it will be, in itself, a great service to humanity. In a period when deception is a high art, truth becomes a vital and precious commodity. Our mission of building peace should ask us as a minimum to seek and speak the truth. Certainly, Jesus did that. The Bible calls us to no less.

5. The Magnificat and Mars Hill

"PEACE IS A WORLD. . .IN WHICH JUSTICE CAN BE OB-TAINED. . .AND CONFLICT RESOLVED THROUGH NONVIOLENT PROCESSES. . . ." What kind of justice does the Bible envision? One beautiful expression of hope is found in the Magnificat. Mary summarizes many Old Testament passages in her poignant and flowing poem. From Habakkuk, I Samuel, Genesis, Psalms, Ecclesiasticus, Ezekiel, Isaiah, Micah and II Samuel, Mary gathers up the words which tell of God's mighty power to support the weak and bring them to their fullest expression (Luke 1:46-55 RSV):

My soul magnifies the Lord, and my spirit rejoices in God my savior, for he has regarded the low estate of his handmaiden. For behold, all generations will call me blessed; for he who is mighty has done great things for me, and holy is his name. And his mercy is on those who fear him from generation to generation. He has shown strength with his arm, he has scattered the proud in the imagination of their hearts, he has put down the mighty from their thrones, and exalted those of low degree; he has filled the hungry with good things, and the rich he has sent empty away. He has helped his servant Israel, in remembrance of his mercy, as he spoke to our fathers, to Abraham and to his posterity forever.

Mary's beautiful phrases, each like a flower, come together in a bouquet and stand as a passionate statement of the hope of the marginal for their rightful chance at fairness in the human experience. Mary's song says, in effect, that those with advantage shall lose their advantage and the lowest ones will take their place. Mary's vision of a time in which fairness is established by a reversal of the existing order speaks authentically to many in the Christian family outside the U.S. and Canada.

In the report from a workshop held in the Philippines by the former East Asia Christian Conference (now Christian Conference of Asia) on the topic "Theology in Action" the delegates noted this about the Magnificat: "We read Mary's outburst carefully. . .(and) in our mission of Magnificat theology, we invite all (persons) of good will to work with us. We do not monopolize the promise of the Magnificat as though it is our holy, private property. We want to see all (persons) of faith come into the field of the Magnificat vision." The commitment to the establishing of Magnificat-fairness is a driving force for many Christians in other places. It is a vision which obviously gives hope and life and courage. That the Magnificat plays such a relatively inconsequential role in North American theology shows us a glimpse of the fact that we have much to learn from and about our Christian family in many lands.

This should point us to another element in our mission of building peace: namely, to discover the theological richness in the Asian, African and Latin American nations. In such nations, persons often struggle for their lives on a day-by-day basis. A theology marked by smugness or pride or power just doesn't speak to their reality. When our North American theology has those elements to it, as it is sometimes apt to do at prayer breakfasts, we need to be reminded that we are doing our theology in quite limited cultural terms. We are under constant temptation to explain our national ventures into global power struggles as though they were exercises in living out the gospel. Our reference point in the world should more readily be our Christian brothers and sisters and what they are saying than it should be the conventional wisdom of those in power.

There is a corollary to the Magnificat theology which other churches know, too. In Asia, Africa and Latin America where, combined, at least a baker's dozen of repressive regimes exist, our colleagues are quite clear that to challenge the existing distribution of power and authority will cause them to suffer. They turn to I Peter 5:8-11 and 4:12 and remind themselves of the New Testament advice (Oxford Annotated):

> Beloved, do not be surprised at the fiery ordeal which comes upon you to prove you, as though something strange were happening to you. But rejoice in so far as you share Christ's sufferings. . . . Humble yourselves therefore under the mighty hand of God, that in due time he may exalt you. Cast all your anxieties on him, for he cares about you. Be sober, be watchful. Your adversary the devil prowls around like a roaring lion, seeking someone to devour. Resist him, firm in your faith, knowing that the same experience of suffering is required of your brotherhood throughout the world. And after you have suffered a little while, the God of all grace, who has called you to his eternal glory in Christ, will himself restore, establish, and strengthen you.

Venture Out There and See

This is a true word of great promise for many in Korea, Chile, Zimbabwe (Rhodesia), Brazil, the Philippines and other places who must live under the unfair use of law. It is when this passage is looked at over against our use of I Peter in the U.S. and Canada, however, that we see how much we need the shared insights of the Christian family in other places. We are likely to turn to the third chapter of I Peter 3:1-2 (if we use it at all) and see: "Likewise you wives, be submissive to your husbands, so that some, though they do not obey the word, may be won without a word by the behavior of their wives. . .when they see your reverent and chaste behavior." Our eyes see what this culture prepares them to see. Why would we come to the blunt commentary on the necessity of suffering and see instead the language of submission and obedience? I do not mean to labor the I Peter passage too much: the larger point should stand out that we need the interaction of our family around the world if we are going to see the relevance of the gospel word to our world setting. Fortunately, new lines of communication are opening all the time.

Biblical encounter across national lines will lead us to one other area. When we listen to Christians in other sectors of the world, we discover that they are using their theology face-to-face with persons of other living faiths. Muslims, Hindus, Buddhists and Shintoists, for example, also have deep commitments to peace and justice. Their traditions have long wrestled with the same issues which stand before the Christian community. Of course, perspectives differ. We are not all saying the same thing. But, grounds for common cooperation do exist, and persons in other Christian families are finding and cultivating them. There are Christian persons in the U.S. and Canada, for example, who sincerely feel that our faith will be lost, watered-down or even washed-out if we enter into dialogue with other faiths. They feel that the uniqueness of the Christian gospel will be lost and that to be the particular generation that "sells out" to them is unacceptable. The conclusion frequently following this extremist position is that we should not seek dialogue at all. But the Christian family in many places is telling us that we simply don't have the luxury of avoiding dialogue. Quite to the contrary, they seem to be saying that the integrity of faith is enhanced and made more visible only when it is tested with other faiths. From Paul on Mars Hill to the World Conference of Religions for Peace in Louvain, Belgium, in 1974, the plain fact stands out: Christianity thrives on encounter with the real world of other faiths and other ideologies. Whether we feel comfortable with this is not the point. A global village requires communication at this deepest level and the rest of the Christian family is taking that seriously whether we are equipped to or not. The mission of building peace will require an understanding of the uniqueness of our faith and its great subtleties if we are going to participate in a world that has the capacity to respect differences and to appreciate uniqueness.

In any case, the promise is that God is not without a witness in any period of history. We do not know what the character of that word and that witness might be, but we do know that God will be there and that the world is conveyed to us for responsible participation. Lest we sell short such a risky, wonderful promise, we must find the ways to hear God out there beyond us, the God who, as in the post-Easter narrative, has gone ahead of us to Galilee.

6. The Jubilee Blueprint

Two other biblical images, not directly included in the definition of peace used in this book, but nonetheless important building blocks in the work of peace, are Jubilee and Shalom.

Leviticus 25:11-34 summarizes the four happenings of the Year of Jubilee: the land is to be left fallow for a year, debts are to be remitted, slaves are to be liberated and family property holdings are to be returned to each individual in the family if they are being held by someone else. Coming only every 50 years, it restores all legal and financial advantage to the fairness provided in the law of holiness. It is a time of restored relationships and new possibilities. While it is unrealistic to pretend that the ancient law of Israel resembles English common law and its variations today, we can still observe the deep sense of fairness and concern for persons embodied in that ancient law. We can look at it symbolically as a word for our time, as Jesus did in his later teachings.[1]

Lessons of the Jubilee

Take a symbolic look at the four categories of the Year of Jubilee. Letting the land lie fallow to restore itself was one requriement of Jubilee. The contemporary concern for the restoration of land ought to inform our own mission of building peace. All over the world the low esteem placed on rural development and agriculture causes us to wish that we had paid attention to these areas in our headlong rush, as a world, to engage in industrial development. For we now realize that industrial development can only be sustained in a nation built on a solid rural foundation. Where silence or ignorance previously ruled out this fact, we must now speak and know. Part of our mission of building peace is to assert the validity and the urgency of rural development. This is symbolized for us in the Year of Jubilee. We need to ask, however, whether a new priority on rural development truly addresses the same issue of unfairness in land distribution. In some developing nations, rural development means the enhancement of the wealth and prestige of those who currently hold the land. They benefit from land improvement schemes while tenant farmers stay the same. The marginal remain marginal. A recent background paper prepared for consideration by the National Council of Churches' group working on a Hunger Policy Statement presented a fresh view on this problem:

"The land is mine" (Leviticus 25:23) says the Lord. The Bible is replete with evidence of the custodial relationship with God in regard to land. It also condemns the control of land by the few. "Woe to those who . . . add field until there is no more room." (Isaiah 5:8) We must not give religious endorsement to unlimited ownership of land by individual and corporate landlords while countless peasants are landless. Perhaps, in this 200th anniversary of America, Christians should re-examine the ancient Hebrew law of "Jubilee" by which, on every fiftieth year, land accumulated through debt or by purchase reverted to its original owners. Whoever controls land controls people. According to the Gospel of the Kingdom, human rights must take precedence over property rights. The people's right to a more just distribution of land is God-given.[2]

This statement points to the fact that biblical concern for the land was tampered with the commitment to see the land used justly.

The second aspect of Jubilee sees debts remitted. An example from our time shows why this was important to the establishment of justice. In many parts of the world, high-interest lenders hold liens on the crops worked by peasants. This results in the peasant actually working for the money-lender who is usually also the grain merchant who at harvest time takes the crop in return for debt at the very low-

est price. Christian peasant communities in various places have joined hands to extricate themselves from debt of this kind. They know that the endless cycle of poverty will not change until it is broken by common action. They support each other financially and thereby work for fairness and economic justice.

There is another current example of the remission of debts which needs to be experienced by our human family. Think what it would mean if the world could be relieved of its massive indebtedness to war. International arms trade and military preparation cost the human family over a quarter of a trillion dollars each year. Given the terrible poverty and hunger in the world, it is cheap and petty to justify this kind of trade as "good business." Higher concerns, values and loyalties should inspire a Christian community which claims to represent a faith transcending national boundaries, and which needs to start thinking beyond the agenda of any one nation. The Year of Jubilee symbolizes an end to overwhelming debt. Can we hear that promise and understand what it could mean to us? And can we act to put an end to the extraordinary misplacement of priorities which keeps us in bondage to our arms?

Slaves liberated as part of the third requirement of the Year of Jubilee were slaves because of their poverty. The liberation that Jubilee brought eliminated a social problem and restored productive persons to a place of fairness, citizenship. Today's poor, slaves of insolvency, are like those in ancient Israel who were outside the mainstream. The slogan "the poor pay more" is well known, but it also happens to be true. As we begin the mission of building peace, we must understand and act to put an end to the economic unfairness that takes advantage of people's impoverished status. The church doesn't have much inside knowledge about how Most Favored Nations are selected in international trading. Often we don't know the details about the tax preferences and conditional arrangements that enhance global big business. But we do know the advantage of the wealthy nations is increased with nearly every decision and that the poor seem to get poorer. This has something to do with economic policies and procedures. The habit of developed nations, particularly in the U.S., is to cast slurs about the backwardness of peoples and their inability to manage their economies. We must realize that it is not quite that simple. Preferential laws enacted by our elected representatives are directly contributing to the continuation of both poverty and privilege.

In the mission of building peace, we are required to come to terms with these facts. This means that we must study harder than we have ever studied before and work in ways we haven't yet worked. It is a "cop-out" to say we are not responsible for raising these questions or that these questions are too difficult for the average church member to understand. Such statements, quite frankly, are excuses for not standing up for the marginal and poor who do not have the same voice as the U.S. church in establishing the nation's agenda. The promise of the Year of Jubilee is that other people in other times were able to overcome involuntary poverty. It is not naive to hold out that hope now, "realism" notwithstanding. Who will hold out hope if even those given the rich legacy of the biblical vision will not?

The final requirement of the Year of Jubilee was the redistirbution of wealth in the form of land. Our mission of building peace will require our grappling with the economic facts of life. Redistribution of wealth on a national and international basis must be discussed openly. To discuss means to discover that our allegiance to our economic system is far deeper than our allegiance and commitment to the poor of this world. But whether or not we like it, the world is forcing this question on the developed nations responsible, in too large a part, for wealth gained from the sweat of the poor. It is not enough to defend this economic system by glossing lightly over its contradictions, nor is it enough to respond with the military mindset that all those who wish to redistribute our world's common holdings are enemies of the state. Even if this generation of Americans cannot face this issue honestly, the next generation will not have that choice. Already the tide of world history is moving inevitably to a new international economic order not designed to enhance the well-being of just one or two. Just as Israel came to terms with redistribution in the Year of Jubilee, so now will the U.S., which two centuries ago named itself the "new Israel," have to come to terms with this issue. If we really want to accept the mission of building peace, this task is ours.

The Final Hope

What the Year of Jubilee required of people in Old Testament times was small compared to what the Old Covenant promised them. The Old Covenant, and also the New, both promise the establishment of Shalom. This serves as the major underlying word in speaking about God's purpose with this creation. The creation of the world (cosmos) put an end to chaos. Shalom, characteristic of the cosmos, stood opposed to chaos, or creation with an underlying purpose stood against anarchy. The nature of Sahlom is not easy to translate into English, but generally it means hope, wholeness, fulfillment, well-being and security. The Old Testament idea envisioned God establishing Shalom throughout the creation. All creation was struggling away from chaos toward Shalom, and this larger vision is one way of describing the purpose of God in history. The Bible has dared to claim that Shalom will be established and that chaos and darkness will not triumph. Shalom can also be translated as peace, and it is the claim of the Bible that the establishment of peace is the will of God. Jesus, Prince of Peace, was the continuation of the Old Testament promise that peace would come and be established. That promise is true and not cynical. It will be done.

We desperately need one more building block in our mission of building peace: we need to be able to catch this longer historical vision of Shalom and make it our central loyalty as Christians. Those who mistake the structures of the moment—government, or church, or university, or others—as the final loyalty in history will be bitterly disappointed as such structures act on the basis of lesser visions. Indeed, as a Latin American theologian, Enrique Dussel, has pointed out, Christians ought to act as "atheists" to these lesser gods. To make the enactment of Shalom our central loyalty as Christians in no way removes us from the day-to-day workings of the institutions of the world, but we dare not forget that they are not God. It is only the larger purpose of Shalom which will triumph in history. For those ot us who wish to begin the mission of building peace clinging to the fulfillment of Shalom in history, we have the overwhelming secret now whispered to us: God's word does not return empty. We are going to win!

Part Two

The Shaping of Values and Violence

Sister Luke Tobin

7. A Violent Way of Life

The "peaceful world" defined in the preface and expanded upon by Michael McIntyre rejects both the overt violence of war and the covert violence of unjust systems. Therefore, if we attempt to understand what we are rejecting, we must take a serious look at violence, both overt and covert, and begin to build a value system on "the world of sharing and nonviolent processes."

Overt violence surrounds us. Not only television violence and the savage brutality of many current films, but the wide coverage of real life violence accosts the senses and sensibilities. Even worse, bombings and killings are such commonplace subjects in the media that we react inured to the assault and immune to its implications.

What do we think of when we hear the word "violence"? Robert McAfee Brown, in his book, *Religion and Violence*, relates violence with personhood. "Violare means 'to violate.' Whatever 'violates' another in the sense of infringing upon or disregarding or abusing or denying that other, whether physical harm is involved or not, can be understood as an act of violence. The basic overall definition of violence would then become violation of personhood. While such a denial or violation can involve the physical destruction of personhood in ways that are obvious, personhood can also be violated or denied in subtle ways that are not obvious at all, except to the victim."[3]

Violence: Violation of Personhood

Perhaps it would be helpful to examine some of the ways in which this violation of personhood takes place. Professor Newton Garver has developed a continuum along which we may position four manifestations of violence:[4]

1. The clearest instance of violence is, of course, personal overt physical assault, in which one person does physical harm to another.

2. When overt physical assault is practiced in corporate terms, it becomes institutionalized overt physical assault. The clearest example is war.

3. Personal covert violence takes place when one individual violates the personhood of another in ways that are psychologically

destructive rather than physically harmful.

4. Personal covert violence can become institutionalized covert violence. This occurs when the institutions or structures of society violate the personhood of society's members.

The Violence of War

Our recent and painful experience in Vietnam forces us to ask again and again, "Why?" What is the whole purpose and meaning of war, the most devastating kind of overt violence? How is it that Christians, persons of peaceable persuasion, are so ready to defend the use of arms? By looking back on our history, perhaps we can learn some of the reasons.

What is the New Testament perspective on war? The overall picture puts the burden of proof on those who would use Jesus' life and teaching in order to justify going to war. Not only is it wrong to kill the enemy—even hating the enemy is proscribed. There is a positive command to love and even to pray for the enemy, who may not be the subject of retaliation. If one is smitten on the cheek, the other cheek must be turned. It is not the warmakers, but the peacemakers, who are blessed.

After the early period of Christian communal sharing, so beautifully described in Acts, the attitude toward violence in war could be defined as Christian pacifism. The early Christians, who took very seriously the injunction that they were not to take up the sword, refused to serve in the Roman armies for centuries. Literature from this early period gives ample evidence of the pacifist position of the church.

Before many centuries had passed, however, the church faced the problem of rapid and unexpected growth. Conversions to Christianity followed the Roman Empire's expansion. But, like any advancing conqueror, the emperor met resistance. A decision to admit the contained use of arms resulted from the confrontation of Constantine with the pagan North. Christian teaching decided on the use of arms for self-protection and self-defense wherever "the enemy" was met.

Later, the "just war" theory developed from the teaching of St. Augustine, and formed the basis for Christian teaching on war for centuries to come. This theory holds that a war can be considered

43

just only if the following conditions are present: It must be declared by a legitimate authority; must be carried out with a right intention; must be undertaken only as a last resort; must be waged on the basis of the principle of proportionality; must have a reasonable chance of success; must be waged with all moderation possible.

This theory seemed acceptable to Christians if conditions were ever such that it was possible to "reflect reasonably" before taking to combat. But by no stretch of the imagination can the "just war" theory be applied to modern war. Any theory that would tolerate nuclear warfare would be immoral because, by its very nature, nuclear warfare deals death and destruction to whole populations. Who can think of a dispute that could be settled by no other means?

With the ending of the war in Vietnam, Americans began to hear others vocalize the futility of war. Commented *The New Yorker* (May 12, 1975): "Our emotions had to be reflective ones: regret at the irredeemable waste of our efforts; relief that it was all over." And *The Saturday Review* (May 3, 1975) editorialized employing a question-and-answer method: Question—"Is anything to be learned from the terrible tragedy of Indo-China, a tragedy that has taken an estimated 1,600,000 lives of Vietnamese and 56,000 lives of Americans?" Answer—"American people, historically, have always been committed to the principle of self-determination. The moment we violated our tradition in this respect we set the stage for a series of escalating miscalculations. . . . If we have learned anything at all from Vietnam, it is that American security does not depend on secret police or undercover agents playing the international game of subversion and intrigue. It depends primarily on the creation of instruments of world order."

Regardless of what reasons have incited a country to conflict, reflection on the characteristics of war gives some insight into its futility and violence:

Wars escalate within themselves. Even when armies march off to wrest power from the evil oppressor, the desperation generated by the intransigence of the foe leads to greater violence. In World War II, the point was reached when the concept of the incalculable destruction of the atomic bomb was first tolerated, then implemented.

Wars brutalize. Who does not remember the callousness of the famous remarks so many of us tossed off in discussions during the Vietnamese War: "The only way to save the city is to destroy it." "Asians don't put the same value on life as we do." "We were told to 'waste' the area, so we killed them."

Wars incite emotions that overpower reason. This creates an atmosphere of blind trust in leaders, making it less likely that citizens will participate in government, and more likely that the government will act in a secret and arbitrary manner.

Wars leave behind a legacy of hatred. Long sequences of enmity and hostility follow wars, which lead to new wars. We shall see later, when we consider the spiral of violence, that the hostility of one war generates another, as in World Wars I and II. Violence never heals.

Surely recent experience has resoundingly demonstrated that nothing short of the most evident kind of defense need should be allowed to provoke us into using the machinery of violence which is war. To quote Professor Brown: "When we look at war as 'the most obvious example of violence' we are reminded more forcefully than ever of the less obvious examples of violence that surround us whether we are in the midst of war or not. . . . Our attempt to force a small country into submission in Asia is a reminder of our attempt to force small groups (Indians, Puerto Ricans, Chicanos) into submission here at home. . . . The violence that takes place in war is only an exaggerated reminder of the violence that takes place in the rest of our society."[5]

Structural Violence

While violence on the massive scale of war is, of course, the most heinous illustration of overt violence, violence in the cities is also present before our eyes. Because the many examples of physical violence appearing in the media seem to strike close to home, we tend to judge violence in terms of the individual, the physically disturbing, the personally frightening. The violence we want to see restrained is the violence of the mugger waiting for us on the parking lot or in the elevator. This is reasonable, of course, but it can shift our attention away from a wider concept of violence. It can make us unable to

ST. AUGUSTIN'S "JUST WAR THEORY"(*)

1. IT MUST BE DECLARED BY A LEGITIMATE AUTHORITY

WHAT IS A LEGITIMATE AUTHORITY WILL BE DETERMINED BY DECREE

2. IT MUST BE CARRIED OUT WITH A RIGHT INTENTION

IT IS OUR RIGHT AND INTENTION TO GUARANTEE OUR INVESTMENTS ABROAD BY HELPING TO DE-STABILIZE LEGITIMATE GOVERNMENTS AND REPLACING THEM BY FRIENDLY ONES HOWEVER BLOODY

(*) SEEN AGAINST TODAY'S NEWS...

3. IT MUST BE UNDERTAKEN ONLY AS A LAST RESORT

THAT IS, IF AFTER SENDING CIA AGENTS, TRAINING LOCAL POLICE ON TORTURE TECHNIQUES, EQUIPPING REPRESSIVE FORCES WITH MODERN WEAPONS, BRIBING AND CORRUPTING LOCAL GOVERNMENT OFFICIALS, FINANCING STRIKES, FUNDING LOCAL "FRIENDLY" NEWSPAPERS, PARTIES ETC 'IF AFTER ALL THAT EFFORT WE DIDN'T SUCCEED IN TOPPLING THEM, THEN IT'S WAR!

4. IT MUST BE WAGED ON THE PRINCIPLE OF PROPORTIONALITY

WE KEEP IT STRICTLY PROPORTIONAL TO THE NET PROFITS OF THE ARMAMENT INDUSTRY

5. IT MUST HAVE A REASONABLE CHANCE OF **SUCCESS**

WE HAD IT: WE HAD
THE MOST POWERFUL
WAR MACHINE THE
WORLD HAS EVER
SEEN — WE THOUGHT
WE'D SUCCEED...

BUT
THERE WAS A DETAIL
<u>THEY</u> WERE
RIGHT...

SO...

6. IT MUST BE WAGED WITH ALL THE MODERATION POSSIBLE

THE WEAPON I'M
RESEARCHING WILL
MEET THIS DEMAND —
MODERATE PRODUCTION
COSTS PER
MAXIMUM KILLING
CAPACITY!

appreciate the far greater problem of the more organized presence of violence on a massive and corporate pattern.

The crime that breaks out of the ghetto reflects the result of the injustices forcing people to live in the ghetto in the first place. Serious questions about our society are raised when the lives of children in Harlem, New York City, for example, are blighted so early that healthy development is stunted. Ned O'Gorman, a school teacher in Harlem, tells his shock to see the hatred in the eyes of a teen-ager who previously had been one of his most alert and responsive pupils.[6]

The structures and institutions of our country contain within themselves elements that do violate the personhood of many of those within the society. In our slums we have seen the vicious cycle of deprivation of healthy human growth. Physical want, decay, poor schools (resulting in poor preparation for jobs) perpetuate themselves. All of this means "violation of personhood," and is a clear example of structural violence. Harlem is a graphic example of conditions resulting from the perverse use of power in many places throughout the world. Structural violence, we see, happens not just to a few of the human family, but to the great majority. It is difficult to contend that violence is not being exercised in a world which Barbara Ward terms "lopsided," and where such conditions as the following exist:

• two-thirds of the population have insufficient food to eliminate hunger,

• the lowest third of the world's population in the least developed nations are in danger of starvation,

• the success of "the green revolution," picked up more fully in Part Three of this book, has been aborted by the need for fertilizer (oil-based), water, research and agricultural training,

• raw materials extracted from Third World nations are returned, and processed for sale in those same nations at a cost many times that of the source material.

To restrict people in such a way that they have no hope of escaping their condition is an unjust exercise of force. Those who in some way participate in this kind of oppression—and perhaps profit by it—are exercising violence regardless of whether or not they preach in the name of peace. Laws which maintain the kind of order condemned by Martin Luther King, Jr. as "moral means to an immoral end" are in fact instruments of violence and oppression. Blind destruction on the part of the oppressed is, of course, futile and immoral; but can we condemn a desperation we have helped to cause? Emmanuel Mounier once said, "People think too much about acts of violence, which prevents them from seeing that more often there are states of violence—as when there are millions of men out of work and dying and being dehumanized, without visible barricades and within the established order today—and that just as the tyrant is the real subversive, so real violence, in the hateful sense of the word, is perpetuated by such a system."[7]

Violence Spirals

Violence never stands alone; it is always caused, and is always followed with effects. A brief but powerful description of the process by which violence is caused, and produces in its turn revolt and repression, is given succinctly by Archbishop Dom Helder Camara, Catholic archbishop of Recife, Brazil.[8] He feels that the basic form of violence, which he calls Violence No. 1, is injustice. This is similar to what we have just described as the hidden or covert violence that does not necessarily do direct physical harm, but is nonetheless a "violation of personhood." It is the subtle, institutionalized destruction of human possibilities that constantly occurs, but is often not apparent to those comfortably situated. It is present whenever the structures of society act so as to depersonalize people by making them objects of action rather than subjects.

This "established" violence, Violence No. 1, attracts Violence No. 2, which is revolt. Revolt may come from the oppressed themselves. Or it may come from youth, firmly resolved to battle for a more just and humane world. The victims of injustice, for example, finally decide that they must throw off the shackles of their oppression and end the massive injustice they have suffered. The place to focus attention is not on Violence No. 2, revolt, but on the basic cause of the violence, which is, as Dom Helder reminds us, found in Violence No. 1, injustice. It is because of the injustices of our society that the spiral of violence initially is launched, and until and unless we get at the roots of injustice, we will be dealing in only a superficial way with the problem of violence. As Dom Helder puts it, "The only true answer to violence is to have the courage to face the injustices which constitute Violence No. 1."

Just as Violence No. 1, injustice, leads to Violence No. 2, revolt, so does Violence No. 2 lead to Violence No. 3, which Dom Helder calls repression. Confronted with revolt, those who hold power put down the revolt by whatever repressive means are necessary to ensure that their power is not threatened. "The authorities consider themselves obliged to preserve or re-establish public order," continues Dom Helder, "even if this means using force; this is Violence No. 3. Sometimes they go even further, and this is becoming increasingly common. In order to obtain information, which may indeed be important to public security, the logic of violence leads them to use moral and physical torture—as though any information extracted through torture deserved the slightest attention!"

Dom Helder continues, "If violence is met by violence, the world will fall into a spiral of violence." One might conclude at this point that the kind of violence Dom Helder is talking about exists only in the Third World, from which he comes. But this same structural violence can be detected in our own nation and in the covert violence underlying some developed nations' activities in the Third World.

Structural Violence in the U.S.

Let us look at some examples of structural violence in the U.S. or in countries which we influence. But first, take a look at home. The deteriorating condition of the Appalachian poor surfaced to public attention during the long congressional debate on strip mining. The plight of persons living in Appalachia was graphically described by the Appalachian Catholic bishops in a message entitled "Powerlessness in Appalachia," released early in 1975.[9] Tracing the oppressive situation in Appalachia, the document describes the early effects of strip mining under absentee landowners:

> There is a saying in the region
> that coal is king.

That's not exactly right.
The kings are those who control big coal,
and the profit and power
which come with it.
Many of these kings
don't live in the region. . . .

. . . Later on for many people,
whose lives were tied to coal,
the unions didn't matter so much any more.
Coal gave way to oil,
and a different suffering
came across the mountains.

The people from the mountains
fled to the cities
looking for jobs.
But in the cities
the jobs were few. . . .

When foreign oil-producing nations
suddenly became more demanding
on the world market,
giant U.S. business interests
began to plan for
U.S. "energy independence."
One way to do that
was to go back
to a half dead and forgotten past,
to coal.

But the new power,
which a return to coal
could bring to Appalachia,
would probably not make its people
any more powerful.
Instead, they would live
a different kind of powerlessness,
one common to the rest of our society,
the powerlessness of isolated little people
in the face of the most powerful corporate giants
on this earth.

> The driving force
> behind this perversion is
> "Maximization of Profit,"
> a principle which too often converts itself
> into an idolatrous power. . . .

> Profit over people
> is an idol.
> And it is not a new idol,
> for Jesus long ago warned us,
> you cannot be the slave
> both of God and money (Matthew 6:24).

The Violence of Racism

Racism in our society is deep-rooted and bitter. The bussing strife is sparked by racist fear. Even though the people actively opposing bussing do not see themselves as racist, nevertheless they collaborate in racial injustice because of the structures which have prevented peaceful integration over the years. Lack of planning, of provisions for fair housing regulations and of proposals for easier transition from neighborhood to neighborhood and from job to job are all defects of government structures, local and national. The United Farm Workers' struggle itself has included racial overtones. The writer remembers the testimony of a former Teamster leader who recalled that notices to workers in canneries were printed only in English and the Chicanos were referred to by management in racist language.

The Violence of Sex Discrimination

Discrimination against women is a widespread and pervasive form of structured violence. Only now are women beginning to discern the lasting and oppressive effects of long centuries of fixed role expectations. Some results are:

1. Legal and economic practices discriminatory against women, are only now beginning to be recognized and challenged.

2. The stereotyping of women as dependent and helpless leads many women to accept this role as advantageous to themselves, thus perpetuating the oppression.

3. Within the church, with its long tradition of male dominance, women have not been accepted for the ministry at all in some denominations; and in others, in spite of ordination, find themselves relegated to secondary positions.

4. Many gifts, talents or potentialities among women remain undiscovered and undeveloped.

5. This evil contributes to the oppression of men as well as women, forcing men into role expectations that deprive them of developing gifts and potentialities in conflict with male stereotypes.

Global Structural Violence

An example of global structural injustice, flowing from U.S. involvement in Latin America, concerns some activities of the Central Intelligence Agency (CIA). Revelations of CIA chief, William Colby, in 1974 regarding funds secretly appropriated between 1970 and 1973 to bribe members of the Congress in Chile, and other acts calculated to destabilize Chile's economy and precipitate military intervention against Chile's elected president, sparked immediate reaction. Rev. William Wipfler, of the Latin America Working Group of the National Council of Churches, responded to these revelations saying: "This is one of the most serious threats to missionary outreach in my entire experience. Every United States missionary is now automatically suspect. The groundwork has been laid for wholesale expulsions of missionaries or at least strict controls on their entry and activities, as occurred in China, India, Ceylon and elsewhere in Asia and Africa after World War II."[10]

Evidence that the CIA conducted illegal activities in Chile and other nations of Latin America and elsewhere elicited a shocked response from press. Stories distributed by the National Catholic News Service and by Religious News Service were widely reproduced. *America* commented editorially, "The American missionary rightly feels betrayed by activities . . . which generate suspicion of the United States and its citizens. Missionaries have a right not to have their efforts undercut by their own government." *New World Outlook*, published by agencies of the United Methodist and United Presbyterian Churches, warned that one cannot "defend democracy by destroying it." As long as U.S. citizens shrug shoulders, romanticize "spy thrillers," and pass the buck to politicians, it added, there will be blood on our hands, "for it is our money and our government that pay for the regimes that do the killing."

Growing consciousness of the economic exploitation of modern indurstrial nations is a new characteristic of our time. The writer remembers very well the anxiety expressed by several Asian women brought together by Church Women United in a Japan, 1974 peace consultation. "Go back and tell your government that they are exploiting us economically, and that, in order to do so successfully, they have been supporting repressive governments."

We have all heard of and read about examples of repression in Communist-dominated countries. However, in that part of the world where U.S. commercial interests and military aid are so influential, we see growing examples of this kind of structural violence. Repressive governments, with their own CIA and torture tactics, now exist in such nations as Chile, Korea, the Philippines and Taiwan. The cycle of Violence No. 3 is gaining ground throughout the world.

8. Winning Over With Nonviolence

"PEACE IS A WORLD. . .IN WHICH JUSTICE CAN BE OBTAINED AND CONFLICT RESOLVED THROUGH NONVIOLENT PROCESSES. . . ." Since this book's working definition of peace speaks of nonviolent processes as a means of conflict resolution, and as has been shown, conflict is built-in by overt and covert injustice, let us examine what we mean by nonviolence and nonviolent processes.

Victims of structural violence include a majority of the human family. As "the wretched of the earth" become conscious of the ways the powerful live, they are increasingly aware that their exploitation is morally outrageous. Paulo Freire has acquainted us with the theory that once the eyes of the poor are opened to the living style of the rich, they will increasingly demand equal advantages.[11]

Robert S. McNamara, head of the World Bank, recounts his journeys into the least developed nations as journeys into misery. "The Upper Volta, for example, a land of disease and want, is the most abandoned country I have ever seen." "For centuries," says McNamara, "stagnating societies and deprived people remained content with their lot because they were unaware that life was really any better elsewhere. Now, the presence of the transistor radio and the television in remote corners of the world dramatizes the disparities in the quality of life. What was tolerable in the past provokes turbulence today. And what else but turbulence can one expect on a planet linked by instantaneous communication but fragmented by conspicuous inequality? It is inconceivable that one-quarter of humanity, moving forward into a self-accelerating affluence, can succeed in walling itself off from the other three-quarters who find themselves entrapped in a self-perpetuating cycle of poverty."[12]

Is it possible to move against powerful structured violence into a more just society? A look at what is meant by nonviolence is in order now. The late Thomas Merton, noted monk, poet and peace-writer, wrote:

> Non-violence is based on that respect for the human person without which there is no deep and genuine Christianity. It is concerned with an appeal to the liberty and intelligence of the person. Instead of forcing a decision upon him from the outside, it invites him to arrive freely at a decision of his own, in dialogue and cooperation, and in the presence of that truth which Christian non-violence brings into full view by its sacrificial witness. The key to non-violence is the willingness of the non-violent resister to fuffer a certain amount of accidental evil in order to bring about a change of mind in the oppressor and awaken him to personal openness and to dialogue.[13]

No modern example in the U.S. is more illustrative of this principle than the words and practice of Martin Luther King, Jr., who from a Birmingham, Alabama jail wrote in April, 1963:

> I am cognizant of the interrelatedness of all communities and states. Injustice anywhere is a threat to justice everywhere. Whatever affects one directly affects all indirectly. . . . Here we are moving toward the exit of the twentieth century with a religious community

largely adjusted to the status quo, standing as a tail light behind other community agencies rather than a headlight leading people to higher levels of justice. . . .Over the last few years I have consistently preached that non-violence demands that the means we use must be as pure as the ends we seek. So I have tried to make it clear that it is wrong to use immoral means to attain moral ends. Not I must affirm that it is just as wrong, or even more so, to use moral means to preserve immoral ends.[14]

Coretta King, a widow of Martin Luther King, Jr., remembers in personal reflection, "To wake up each morning knowing that I might not see Martin when evening came was a constant anxiety. I knew that his dedication to his task would lead him to the risks which might lead to his death."

Christian nonviolence certainly does not encourage or excuse hatred of any classes or groups. Openness, communication, dialogue and responsiveness compose the purpose of nonviolence. The great exemplars of nonviolence in our time have always engaged in dialogue, though the firmness of their positions and their stand for justice have never been in doubt.

Nonviolence is a most exacting form of struggle calling the nonviolent resister to look above all to the good of the human person. This means a dedication to objective truth beyond any defense of one's own interests or even those of one's own group. And yet, there is a subtle temptation to seek the psychological gratification of one's own ideals and principles and therefore an attendant risk of Pharisaism. Thomas à Becket, in T.S. Eliot's play, *Murder in the Cathedral*, debated with himself, fearing that he might be seeking martyrdom merely in order to demonstrate his own righteousness and the king's injustice: "This is the greatest treason, to do the right thing for the wrong reason."

A Christian's basis of violence is the Gospel message of the kingdom of God to which all are summoned. The saving grace of God in the Lord Jesus is proclaimed in the love, openness, simplicity, humility and self-sacrifice of Christians. By expressing a living faith and applying it to the human problems of their time, Christians show the love of God for all people, and by that action make God visibly present in the world. The chief place in which the mode of life taught by

(1) <u>INDUSTRIAL & ENGINEERING CHEMISTRY</u>, 19 AUGUST 1946
(2, 3) <u>NEW YORK TIMES</u>, 27 DECEMBER 1967

CITED BY <u>NARMIC'S</u> <u>WEAPONS FOR
COUNTERINSURGENCY</u>
JANUARY 1970

Christ is detailed is in the Beatitudes. The poor in spirit are those of whom the prophet spoke, who in the last days will be the humble of the earth; that is to say, the oppressed who have nothing upon which to rely and who nevertheless resist evil. They seek justice in the power of truth and of God, not in the power of humans.

Only love can attain and preserve the good of all. Power always protects the good of some at the expense of all the others. Therefore, the nonviolent resister is persuaded of the superior efficacy of love, openness, peaceful negotiation and, above all, truth. Mahatma Gandhi is perhaps the greatest example of nonviolence in our age. He saw that the fully consistent practice of nonviolence demands a solid religious basis both in being and in God. "Non-violent opposition." Gandhi wrote, "is of no avail to those without living faith in the God of love and love for all mankind." He continued: "I could not be leading a religious life unless I identified myself with the whole of mankind, and that I could not do unless I took part in politics. The whole gamut of man's activities today constitutes an indivisible whole. You cannot divide social, economic, political and purely religious work into watertight compartments."[15]

Effects of Nonviolence

Although the immediate, tangible results of nonviolent action are perhaps somewhat limited, their effects have proven powerful. The ability of a Cesar Chavez, whose philosophy is one of nonviolence, to gather about him thousands of supporters in the United Farm Workers' long struggle to secure justice is a case in point. The long marches, the endless hours on strike lines in the fields and boycott lines across U.S. cities, the enduring of police harassment, unjust court orders, and strong-arm Teamster tactics—none of these have dissuaded Chavez and his followers (the workers, the young, church people, some political leaders) from continuing in their slow movement toward justice, always guided by the nonviolent philosophy which Chavez learned from his study of Gandhi.

Nonviolence seeks to "win," not by destroying or even by humiliating the adversary, but by convincing that person, group or interest that there is a higher and more certain common good than can be obtained by bombs and blood. Nonviolence, ideally speaking, tries not to overcome the adversary by winning over him, her or them, but tries to turn that person, gorup or interest from an adversary into a collaborator by winning him, her or them over.

Illustrations of Winning Over with Nonviolence

Is it possible to illustrate such a winning over by concrete and effective examples in our own times? I am well aware that examples such as I will offer are all too few and infrequent, but perhaps the very thing we need to hearten us for the struggle are stories of occasional successes. I hope some of the ensuing illustrations can serve such a purpose.

A very fine example of such a winning over is related in the story told by Hildegard Goss-Mayr regarding the Indians of Paraguay. At a conference of Church Women United, called to deliberate on world order values, Goss-Mayr gave the following account:

The most oppressed group in Paraguay, now under military dictatorship, are the Guarini Indians, who were driven from the land they originally owned and whose present land is very poor. A few years ago, with the help of a few courageous priests, the Guarini discovered, through Freire's insights, that to work for liberation is to see humankind as a whole, to see the need for liberation for the oppressed and for the oppressor.

The problem is how to go about this. If the oppressed use the same means to obtain this new society as the oppressor uses to suppress them, the old disrespect, oppression, police force, etc. are really implanted, and there will be no liberation. How did the Guarini go about this task?

An unjust society can only exist, they reasoned, because there are certain pillars that sustain it. The Guarini identified six such pillars: (1) the church, (2) education and culture, (3) economics, (4) the police, (5) the army, and (6) the only existing political party. Now, these pillars are not abstract things. They are made up of human beings, mostly passive human beings, who because of their position, privileges and profits, function inside these pillars and sustain a system of injustice. Our task as an active minority, the Guarini said, is not to destroy these pillars because we do not have the strength, the arms, the money, the intelligence to fight them. But, because we know that human beings are within these pillars, we can work to win over more and more people so that they no longer sustain the system. If we succeed in removing a few of these pillars, the unjust situation will change.

The first action of the study groups formed by the Guarini for their task was to confront the church. The bishops called them Communists, to which they replied, "Come to our community, come and see how we live." Some did. They went back again and the dialogue continued. Finally, at Christmas, 1971, the Archbishop of Asuncion decided not to remain in his traditional role of holding a seat in the government until the government would grant all the recommendations of the Guarini.

At the same time, the peasants began to attack the educational and cultural pillars. It is better to sit on the floor and be poor, they said, and learn to struggle for justice than to sit in a nice school and learn to be a slave. The peasants built community schools, and children were taught in their own language. The government did not approve of the new schools and the training of the teachers, and so the schools were destroyed. But the people said, "We know that we have to pay a price to be free. We must learn from Christ, who was crucified because he stood against the injustices of his time and attacked the system of exploitation then existing."

Once in a certain district, all the people in whose homes evening meetings had been held were arrested. But the peasants came to their support, staying in front of the city hall for hours in the rain, barefoot, and with no food. This was done in order to provoke a dialogue. Up to now, the Guarini had not been recognized by the government as a political entity. The government tried to do what it always tries to do —divide and conquer. But the peasants insisted on negotiation, and finally the dialogue began. The prisoners were liberated that evening, but the peasant groups were told they would not be allowed to exist. Nevertheless, the people had obtained part of their objective.

A second repression followed, and the people repeated their demonstration in front of the prison. The police began to move on the people with their cars, but the Guarini said they would not leave until the prisoners were freed. They said to the policemen and soldiers, "You agreed to function in this system in order to have your family survive, but you are one of us. You know why we struggle, and you should be on our side." Then the men, women, and children, 800 to 900 of them, lay down on the ground, saying to the soldiers,

"You can move your tanks on us, but before you do, think that this is your brother, your sister, your mother. You can destroy us because what you are doing is already functioning in the system which destroys us." Not one car moved on them. The prisoners were freed.

So the Guarini continue. Their schools still function. Eroding the economic pillar is the main struggle that goes on. The final aim is basic land reform, in which the land will be returned to them. But while they are struggling, they have made some very important decisions about what a new society should be like.

The revolution that has to go on in minds and attitudes is inseparable from the new structures of society. Unless this change of attitude comes, there cannot be structures that respect people. Among the Guarini, all participate in the planning: women, men, and young people. Sharing resources, spiritual, material, and intellectual, has become the greatest contribution to the building of a new society.

Writing shortly before his death in 1968, Thomas Merton spelled out some conditions for Christian nonviolent practice. They are listed below, and to suggest examples of each, examples are drawn from both recent and early history of nonviolence.[16]

1. *"Non-violence must be aimed above all at the transformation of the present state of the world, and it must therefore be free from all unconscious connivance with an unjust and established abuse of power. This poses enormous problems—for if non-violence is too political it becomes drawn into the power struggle and identified with one side or another in that struggle, while if it is totally a-political it runs the risk of being ineffective or at best merely symbolic."*

Dom Helder Camara is known as the champion of the poor and the spokesperson for the Third World. He has courageously taken stands against oppressive systems in Latin America—for example, the powerful interests of the landowners in Brazil. To combat the unjust use of power, Dom Helder has led church-related social action programs and organized Human Rights Days to conscienticize the Brazilian people concerning the lack of human rights under their nation's military regime. He speaks eloquently of the need for non-violence. "To free ourselves from established violence without appealing to armed violence requires us to adopt positive, courageous, dynamic, effective non-violent action. Revolution in depth . . . but not a bloody revolution. The Christian's option is clear: non-violence. Non-violence is to believe more firmly in justice than injustice, in love more than hatred, in truth more than falsehood. Non-violence must walk with its eyes on heaven, but with its feet on the ground."[17]

Dom Helder works through groups of women and men, helping them to devise their own methods of nonviolent direct action, raising their consciousness and using the Gandhi-inspired tools of the strike, the boycott and fasting.

2. *"The non-violent resistance of the Christian who belongs to one of the powerful nations and who is himself in some sense a privileged member of world society will have to be clearly not for himself but for others, that is for the poor and underprivileged."*

Jane Addams, who in 1889 founded Hull House, and with it the concept of social work in the U.S., exemplifies one whose own background placed her not only in a powerful nation but also in the more privileged class within that nation. After finishing college and some professional (medical) school and following European travels, Jane Addams, seeing the needs of the poor immigrants, opened Hull House. The place became a social center; offered classes; housed a kindergarten, a public kitchen for working women to use, cooperative apartments for working girls, and grew into a center of political debate and activities to help conscienticize the lower-class immigrants. In politics, Jane Addams pushed legislation on child labor and on limiting women's working hours. Much of her political activity helped better the lot of poor workers. Hull House has been called "an experimental laboratory in social reform." It was begun by one acutely aware of the needs of people and willing to resist the status quo to improve the people's living and working conditions.

3. *"In the case of non-violent struggle for peace—the threat of nuclear war abolishes all privileges. . . . This means in fact that in this case above all non-violence must avoid a facile and fanatical self-righteousness, and refrain from being satisfied with dramatic self-justifying gestures."*

This characteristic seems exemplified in the experience of Albert Bigelow, former naval commander, who tells of his own insensitivity to the reality of war during World War II and of his subsequent revulsion at the horror of it, occasioned by the dropping of the atomic bomb on Hiroshima.

Bigelow's recounting of his gradual move from this initial rejection of war to his joining the Quakers and his involvement in peaceful resistance activities, which were geared especially against nuclear testing, is low-keyed and undramatic. The culmination of these activities was his participation, in 1958, in the voyage of the Golden Rule (which he captained) into the forbidden nuclear-testing area of the Pacific. He and his crew were arrested and imprisoned in Honolulu. Bigelow writes of his motives for joining in this episode of nonviolent resistance, aimed at stopping the spread of nuclear arms:

I am going because, as Shakespeare said, "Action is eloquence." Without some such direct action, ordinary citizens lack the power any longer to be seen or heard by their government.

I am going because it is time to do something about peace, not just talk about peace.

I am going to witness to the deep inward truth we all know: "Force can subdue, but love gains."[18]

4. *"Perhaps the most insidious temptation to be avoided is one which is characteristic of the power structure itself—this fetishism of immediate visible results. . . .Here the human dignity of nonviolence must manifest itself clearly in terms of a freedom and a nobility which are able to resist political manipulation and brute force and show them up as arbitrary, barbarous, and irrational."*

The long involvement of Mother Mary Jones (who lived from 1830 to 1930) in the U.S. labor movement shows her as one who was willing to wait for visible results. A widowed schoolteacher, Mother Jones became interested in labor problems in the 1880's and remained so for the rest of her life.

The story of her career follows her around the U.S.—from Illinois to West Virginia to New York to Pennsylvania to Colorado to Utah to Alabama to Arizona. She worked tirelessly for the unionizing of miners, for child labor legislation, always immersing herself in the problems of those who suffered brutal working conditions and the oppression of big employers. Unafraid to spend time in jail for the cause of justice, Mother Jones also spent hours comforting and helping the wives and children of miners who were killed or beaten in the early struggles for their rights. Her spirit of patient waiting for results was captured in a dialogue at a congressional hearing in 1910. When Mother Jones was asked for her address, she replied that she lived in the U.S. and that her address was "wherever there is a fight against oppression." When the chairperson persisted in asking about her permanent abiding place, Mother Jones answered, "I abide where there is a fight against wrong." Unselfish compassion and endurance characterized her in her long struggle against oppression.

5. *"Christian non-violence, therefore, is convinced that the manner in which the conflict for truth is waged will itself manifest or obscure the truth. To fight for truth by dishonest, violent, inhuman, or unreasonable means would simply betray the truth one is trying to vindicate. The absolute refusal of evil or suspect means is a necessary element in the witness of non-violence."*

Unusual courage and willingness to stand up for truth were displayed by Oo Chung Lee, president of Church Women United in Korea. Apprehended and detained several times by the Korean "CIA," this brave woman continued to speak out against abuses of the government, such as allowing young women to be inducted into prostitution in the promotion of business projects in Korea. This she did with calm dignity. Asked how she could continue to speak out and incur possible reprisals, she replied, "It is necessary to take risks. Without risk, no growth and progress toward justice is possible."

A simple gesture of truth—the truth that no person may be deprived of a seat on a bus because of her/his race—was performed by Rosa Parks, a black woman in Montgomery, Alabama, December 1, 1955. Her arrest for refusing to give her place on a bus to a newly boarded white was protested in the famous one-day bus boycott of December 5. This led to a new spirit of determination and nonviolent protest by southern blacks in their struggle to end segregation. Love, dignity and refusal to ride the buses until segregation was abolished motivated the people. In a year's time, following a Supreme Court order and consistent nonviolent discipline by black leaders, desegregation became a reality in Montgomery. Rosa Parks had acted the truth.

6. *"A test of our sincerity in the practice of non-violence is this: are we willing to learn something from the adversary? If a new truth is made known to us by him or through him, will we admit it? Are we willing to admit that he is not totally inhumane, wrong, unreasonable, cruel? Our readiness to see some good in him and to agree with some of his ideas (though tactically this might look like a weakness on our part) actually gives us power, the power of sincerity and truth."*

An example of this kind of listening openness and dialogue with the adversary occurred over a several year period in Colorado. There, in November, 1971, members of Clergy and Laity Concerned requested the opportunity to speak with Air Force Academy cadets on "The Moral Aspects of the Continuing Air War in Indochina." Several national religious leaders were scheduled to participate in the discussion. This request was repeatedly made in letters, meetings with the academy superintendent and frequent attempts at very conciliatory dialogue.

"We believe our program would not involve imposing our views on the cadets, but rather would be a program of sharing views that we think would be valuable for both the speakers and the cadets," stated CALC representatives in a letter to the academy personnel.[19] Although that request was denied (and about 30 CALC members were "detained" at the academy when they held a silent witness against the war during academy religious services), nevertheless the attempts at dialogue continued. Gradually, CALC personnel were permitted to talk to the cadets, and in the fall of 1974, Reverend Bill Sulzman, one of the original CALC members, began to give lectures on the morality of war, as part of ethics courses at the academy.

7. *"Christian hope and Christian humility are inseparable. The quality of non-violence is decided largely by the purity of the Christian hope behind it. The Christian knows that there are radically sound possibilities in every person, and believes that love and grace always have power to bring out those possibilities at the most unexpected moments."*

"Lord, I've got to hold steady on to you, and you've got to see me through." These words of Harriet Tubman, born in 1821 and owned by a Maryland slave master, typified her lifelong attitude of hope as she worked quietly as a "conductor" on the underground railroad. Harriet, who herself encountered many dangers in order to escape slavery, first dreamed of saving only her own family. But anyone with black skin began to have a claim on her courage, and to each she spoke of freedom. The slaves waited to hear Harriet Tubman's familiar low song, "Go down, Moses, and tell old Pharaoh to let my people go." In fact, she became known as Moses. A memorial to this brave black woman, erected after her death, said of Harriet Tubman: "With rare courage she led over three hundred negroes up from slavery to freedom and rendered invaluable service as a nurse and spy. With implicit trust in God she overcame every obstacle."

Harriet Tubman led her people to freedom as did the Moses of the song she sang: "Go down, Moses, and tell old Pharaoh to let my people go." Our new understanding of nonviolence goes even further. It reverses the command to pharaoh; it calls upon us to let pharaoh go. There can be no pharaoh unless we create one by submission. There are no pharaohs if there are not people over whom they can exercise power. As a contemporary song, made famous by Roberta Flack, has put it:

Go up, Moses. . . . You've been down too long.
Go up, Moses. . . . Tell your freedom song.
Am I clear this morning, y'all? . . . My people, let Pharaoh go.
You don't need his tricks. You don't need his trinkets.
Let Pharaoh go. . . . Pharaoh doesn't want you. But he needs you.
My people, let Pharaoh go. Without you, there is no Pharaoh.
So all you got to do . . . to let him go . . . is let him go.
Just wake up tomorrow morning and say, "Bye, Pharaoh, honey!"[20]

One of the insights of the nonviolent movement, as expressed by Gene Sharp, is that power or authority is not intrinsic to the power-holder.[21] He points out six ways used by the power-holder to maintain power: (1) authority (the right to command, to be accepted as superior); (2) human resources (the number of persons who obey the ruler, and their proportion in the general population); (3) skills and knowledge of those whom the power-holder rules (and their relationship to the ruler's needs); (4) intangible factors (e.g., psychological attitudes toward submission, sense of mission, an ideology);

(5) material resources (the ruler's control of property, natural and financial resources, etc., and how such control determines power); and (6) sanctions (the use of them, both against the ruler's own subjects and against other rulers).

Sharp remarks that all types of struggle are based on two primary views of the nature of power. The first sees people dependent on the good will, decisions and support of their government or any other hierarchical system. "Go down, Moses, and tell old Pharaoh to let my people go." The second view is the nonviolent analysis of power that sees that if groups or individuals refuse to acquiesce or concur with that kind of political power, the structure will be unable ultimately to continue. As Roberta Flack's "Go Up, Moses" song says, "All you got to do . . . to let him go . . . is let him go."

Illustrations of Force as an Alternative to Nonviolence

Finally, we will look at some examples of those who, having tried all means of overcoming injustice by peaceful ways, have resorted to force. Pushed to the limits by repressive governments, some Christians feel that the only possibility of cracking the wall of violent power is to weaken or crumble it in vulnerable areas by guerrilla tactics. We have seen that only in extremity has Christian teaching through the centuries contenanced the taking up of arms. From *Social Justice and the Latin Churches,* translated by Jorge Lara-Braud:

> Can the Christian participate directly in the struggle against the established legal structures when there is no prospect that these will be transformed through the actions of existing political movements and parties or social pressure groups? In other words, is it lawful for the Christian actively to participate in revolutionary movements that may resort to violence in cases where the goal of social transformation does not appear viable by any other means? . . . A realistic consideration of this problem should bring one to realize that it is not a matter of introducing violence into a society without violence. . . . The already-existent violence results at every moment in hundreds of deaths from hunger, poverty and disease in Latin America and deprives the people of our continent of the basic necessities for living under "human" conditions. This is to say that the legal social order prevents a person from fulfilling the purpose for which one was created, that of reaching human fullness, the true measure of Jesus Christ. . . .

The unequivocal responsibility of the Christian is to point out and unmask all forms of visible or invisible violence, to seek its causes and possible remedies, and to put into practice the solutions found in the light of the Word of God—knowing that the very realism of the Bible leads one to channel action through existing political and social means and social pressure groups and therefore that one's action can be neither perfect nor ideal.[22]

Illustrations of violent resistance in modern times have been brought to our attention from Latin America: Camilo Torres, Colombian priest who set aside his priestly duties to goin the guerrillas —"until I break bread with my brothers after justice has been obtained"—died of bullet wounds in the Colombian mountains. Nestor Paz, youthful teacher in a Bolivian school, joined the guerrillas in action against the military government, and died of starvation in the Andean mountains. His diary, composed mainly of tender and poignant letters to his wife, also reveals a moving Christian faith. Among the passages in it appears the following prayer:

My dear Lord: It's been a long time since I've written. Today I really feel the need of you and your presence. Maybe it's because of the nearness of death or of the relative failure of our struggle. You know I've always tried to be faithful to you in every way, consistent with the fulness of my being. That's why I'm here. I understand love as an urgent demand to solve the problem of the other—where you are.

I left what I had and I came. Maybe today is my Holy Thursday and tonight will be my Good Friday. Into your hands I surrender completely all that I am with a trust having no limits, because I love you. What hurts me most is perhaps leaving behind those I love the most—Cecy and my family—and also not being able to experience the triumph of the people, their liberation.

We are a group filled with authentic humanity, Christian humanity. This, I think, is enough to move history ahead. This encourages me. I love you, and I give to you all that we are, without measure—because you are my Father.

Nobody's death is useless if his life has been filled with meaning, and I believe ours has been. Ciao, Lord, perhaps until we meet in your heaven, that new land that we yearn for so much.[23]

Without judging the motives of those who have chosen desperate

70

alternatives, it is perhaps fair to say that for most Christians the gospel does not seem to point in that direction. The words of Christ sound unequivocal: "Those who take up the sword shall perish by the sword" (Matthew 26:52). Yet the nature and difficulty of the struggle appeal with equal force to that other hard saying, not to be slighted: "The kingdom of heaven suffers violence and the violent bear it away" (Matthew 11:12). Unhappily, most of us do not display the persevering courage necessary for the nonviolent choice.

Prayer is always the Christian response to the sensing of a call to courageous action and here, above all, is prayer appropriate. For only in an atmosphere of prayer can the Christian, following the example of Jesus, seek to place his or her own convictions and decisions in the presence of One who summons the Christian to uncompromising love of one's brothers and sisters, even in a situation of violence.

9. Forming Values Based on Peaceful Priorities

The importance of our value choices and our selection of moral priorities converge at the point of the value and dignity of the human person in society. If any one thing should be clear after reflecting on the examples of violent and nonviolent alternatives in the previous chapter, it is the emerging of the importance of the value of the human person. Who can describe the mystery, the wealth of potentiality, the incalculable treasury of known and unknown that is a human person? We are describing someone who is not interchangeable with any other. Each person has unique worth. In no legitimate way can we assert that one person is worth more than another, for the worth of each is infinite. As Christians, we hold that no value supersedes that of the infinite worth of the human person in the eyes of God. Parable after parable in the Gospels demonstrates this truth. Further, the value selection of Jesus is evident in his willingness to undergo persecution and hostility as a result of his stand for persons: "The Sabbath was made for man, not man for the Sabbath." Here even the

71

religious laws were to give way to the value of persons.

But the human process of developing values, selecting them, prioritizing and finally acting from them is a lifetime process, complex and filled with uncertainties and vagaries. Is there some way of developing and clarifying our values? Before we can sort out our own value priorities and those of our local and national communities, perhaps we can with profit turn our attention to some of the current processes of value clarification gaining prominence. Brian Hall, in his recent book, *Value Clarification as Learning Process*, sets out some characteristics of this approach.[24]

What Is Value?

What is value? It is a reality at the very center of a person's existence which is basically and uniquely one's own and affects one's behavior, shapes one's ideas and conditions one's feelings. As such, it is a life stance which a person has freely chosen from alternatives and has acted upon, and which the individual celebrates as being part of the creative integration of one's development as a person. One's values are continually developing. They can never be static, but must constantly be rechosen as the person continues to grow. As a person grows in identity and interdependency, he/she is continually choosing values and fashioning his/her hierarchy of values.

The authors of *Values and Teaching* describe seven aspects of a true value. These seven aspects may be divided into three categories: choosing, prizing and acting.

In the area of choice, it is stated that the value must be chosen freely. There must be no coercion; the person makes a free choice and is totally accountable for that choice. Secondly, the choice must be made from alternatives. If there were not any alternatives, then there would be no free choice in the first place; one would only be able to accept what one was faced with. Thirdly, this choice is a thoughtful consideration of the consequences of each alternative. Choices made without thought would not constitute a valuing process.

The second category is prizing. A value that has been chosen should be prized and cherished. The person who chooses a value must be happy about the choice and hold it as something dear. After we have chosen something from the alternatives and are proud of it, we are now glad to be associated with it and are willing to affirm this choice publicly.

The third category of a value is the decision to act upon our choice. One way in which we can check the authenticity of what we say is a value to us, is simply to ask the question: "Have I acted upon it or was it something I was still thinking about?" In this case, for instance, if the person has not acted upon it, it would simply not be a value. There must be commitment—action that changes behavior and makes evident to other people that there is a value present. Finally, the value should be repeatedly acted upon.

The summary of this definition of a value is as follows:

CHOOSING: 1. to choose freely;

                  2. to choose from alternatives; and

                  3. to choose from alternatives after considering the consequences of each alternative.

PRIZING: 4. cherishing and being happy with the choice; and

                  5. willing to affirm the choice publicly.

ACTING: 6. actually doing something with the choice; and

                  7. acting repeatedly in some pattern of life.[26]

Value clarification is a methodology or process by which a person is helped to discover one's values through behavior, through feelings, through ideas—what important choices one has made. To live on a set of values assimilated from one's upbringing rather than chosen is to move in directions and to have goals that are hidden from oneself, of which one is not aware. It is only as one, as an adult, clarifies what choices have a major influence on one's personality, that one can really understand who one is and where one is going.

Choosing Value Systems

Realizing that hope for the future lies in the young people who will soon be the decision-makers holding the world's destiny in their power, one comes to hope that the value systems they are forming are directed toward peace. How can children and youth learn to become creative, nonviolent social agents in a complex world if they are not forming sound values based on peaceful priorities? And how can we as adults be witnesses for youth of such values in the search for peace? How can I tell, for example, if I have incorporated into my own priority system the value of the human person and his/her basic needs, so paramount in the search for peace? "Peace is a world where human needs are met, . . .and material resources are shared for the benefit of all people." What is peace in my life? Do choosing, prizing and acting help me to arrive at peace values?

In relating values to persons, here are some questions that one can ask oneself: Do I appreciate the uniqueness, difference and individuality of others? Is this evidence of human dignity? Am I free enough, internally and externally, to develop my own talents and capabilities, and do I want to make it possible for others to do the same? Do I want others to have enough to enjoy the simple, good things of life?

In relating values to world systems and the needs of the wider human community, here are some questions: Do I prize a time, and work for it, when social justice will be more operative in my city? state? nation? world? Do I study the workings of oppressive systems when they are operating; for example, through maltinational corporations? in the military-industrial complex? in foreign trade? in racial and sexual discrimination? in tax systems? Do I take active means to overcome the injustices thus revealed? Am I willing to direct my energies to alleviating world hunger, caused by situations in which, for example, the U.S., with 6 percent of the world's population, consumes 40 percent of the world's goods? What actions does this discrepancy suggest?

Values and Moral Development

Clarifying values according to moral issues is the particular work of Lawrence Kohlberg.[27] Following our identification of the value of the human person, we can receive further help from Kohlberg. He tells us that an individual's thinking about moral situations matures according to a specific sequence that he presents in three levels:

Level 1: Pre-Conventional: At this level an individual's moral reasoning results from the consequences of actions (punishment, reward, exchange of favors) and from the physical power of those in positions of authority.

Level 2: Conventional: At this level an individual's moral reasoning involves consideration of the interests of others (family and peers) and a desire to maintain, respect, support and justify the existing social order.

Level 3: Post-Conventional: At this level an individual's moral reasoning incorporates moral values and principles that have validity and application beyond the authority of groups. Moral reasoning becomes more comprehensive and reflects universal principles. In this last stage, decisions result from an obligation to ethical principles that apply to all humanity. The universal principles of justice, reciprocity, equality of human rights and respect for the dignity of human beings as individuals serve as a basis for individual reasoning.

Kohlberg's studies establish a clear relationship between chronological age and the level of reasoning. Although children and adolescents move at varying rates of speed through the stages, pre-adolescents usually attain a pre-conventional level, adolescents achieve the conventional level and adults move toward the post-conventional level of reasoning. Individuals can, however, become "frozen" at any level. Actually, studies indicate that less than 20 percent of the adult population reasons at the post-conventional level.

The research of Kohlberg and his colleagues has also established that those who participate regularly in discussions of moral dilemmas often begin to articulate reasoning at higher stages of development. This evidence indicates that exchange of reasoning during a group discussion of a moral dilemma can stimulate moral development through the stages. It is thus possible to envisage a growing development of a mature attitude toward peace (universal justice, reciprocity, equality and respect for human dignity) nurtured and encouraged by the process of reasoning through moral dilemmas. For example, during the Vietnam War, some individuals experienced a value development in the area of peace specifically because they took part in actual antiwar activities, demonstrations, prayer meetings and peace marches.

If one places the value of the human person above all other values, how does one confront dilemmas in which persons and laws protecting persons are at variance? in which persons and institutions clash? in which persons with differing values are in conflict? Some examples of such dilemmas readily come to mind: conscientious objection to military service, "lifeboat ethics" in a hungry world, asylum for those whose actions for social justice have brought them into conflict with the law, and integration of neighborhoods.

A few anecdotes will illustrate situations of value development in the experience of some individuals and groups in the area of peace and justice.

• During the Vietnam War, a young man gradually reached the decision that, in conscience, he could not bear arms in a war he saw as unjust. Only after the young man had spent two years in Canada did his father, a highly patriotic man who had resisted his son's decision, visit him. The two spent a long vacation, hunting, fishing and discussing the issue of conscientious objection. When the father returned to his family, he said, "He was right and I was wrong." Reconciliation came only after the father had reassessed his own values and had come to appreciate the value choices of his son.

• A chaplain at a Boy Scout jamboree reflected on the discrepancy he felt between the peace values he was promoting in his daily relationships with Scouts and the military values being implicitly taught through camp activities. Demonstrations of life-saving, first aid and water safety were modelled on military style and frequently assisted by military personnel from a nearby installation. Personal models or "heroes" held up to participants tended to be "200 percent American" rather than international figures, and men identified with the military rather than with peacemaking. In cases like this, how does a young person have his peace values reinforced?

• Honorary membership in an American religious congregation of women was extended to Cao Thi Que Huong, a political prisoner in South Vietnam. Since 1971, she and her husband (who died in prison) had been jailed for speaking out against the military policy of the Thieu regime and for engaging in peace activities. To grant such a membership and to invite the woman to this country (as this religious order did) meant a stand against the U.S. alliance with Thieu and a stand against U.S. support of the repression for which the Vietnamese political prison system became notorious. It meant a group valuing of Huong's personal values of courageous resistance in the cause of peace.

aid often means preventing changes that are required

aid
military or else

• A young American woman reflects on time she spent in Vietnam:

What became clear to me as I observed foreigners working there was that many were indeed operating out of concern, but were not being reflective about how they were helping the Vietnamese. If our goal is a just world in which people have the choice to create their own lives and life directions, how does that goal relate to the services we provide for a people? The work done by most foreigners in Vietnam was paternalistic; the natives were to be served but not consulted in the whole process. For example, orphanages were often directed by foreigners, and all the workers were Vietnamese (with no responsibilities or opportunities to make suggestions). . . .

My experience with the Buddhist School for Social Service

team, which worked with resettling the natives, was in stark contrast to the above situation. The Buddhist monks and nuns lived the life of the people, who were actively involved in naming their own needs and suggesting solutions for their lives. . . .

During a trip to a village with this Buddhist group, I became very ill with dysentery and was attacked by a swarm of bees. A Vietnamese woman took me to the small hut where she and her husband lived, gave me their bed, brought me medicine for the bee stings and soothing soup for my stomach. All they had in their hut were two changes of clothes, mosquito nets, a hat and one cup. I was very humbled by the kindness of this woman who had lived through war, had lost her home and had no material resources.

The experience made the young woman aware of how presumptuous we sometimes become about serving others. We forget that justice has to do with all people giving and receiving.

Examples of developing peace values, like those preceding, serve to reinforce the ability of persons to choose over individual and corporate vested interests.

Our reflections have led us through those considerations of our definition of peace, particularly as it is concerned with violence, non-violence and its processes, the development of our own value system and the importance of peace as a value. We have examined the futility and destructiveness of war. We have seen how the spiral of violence is fed, and how nonviolent action has led to limited, but sometimes remarkable success. We have looked at examples from the lives of nonviolent resisters, and have seen how it is possible to grow toward an ever more profound development of peace values in our own lives. We have seen that when reconciliation becomes possible, difficult as it is, the road to peace-building is enormously smoothed.

Clearly, the movement from violence to nonviolence does not come automatically or without pain. There operates within us a latent resistance to tension, and tension is inevitable for one who would hasten the coming of God's kingdom founded on the cross of Christ. The task of creating a just and peaceful society imposes enormous demands on us, and only by the mutual upholding of one another in the process of choosing life over death can we respond, with any adequacy, to the liberating call of Christ.

Part Three

The Interrelationship Between Peace-Related Issues

Hazel T. Johns

10. Meeting Basic Human Needs

In a recent survey taken in Japan, fifth and sixth grade children were all asked the same question: "Do you think humanity will perish in your lifetime?" The answer was an overwhelming "yes." That belief makes a difference.

Mr. Soedjatmoko, former Ambassador of Indonesia to the U.S., once said: "It is a man's vision of the future, his hopes, fears and expectations that determine his actions in the present." But what if there is no vision of the future? Surely with no vision, no hope, the here and now becomes all important. Live now, never mind tomorrow. "Let us eat and drink for tomorrow we die" (Isaiah 22:13). There will be no future generations. But in the same book of Isaiah are the words ". . .come to the waters; and he who has no money, come, buy and eat" (Isaiah 55:1). Civilization receives its energy from its hopes, not its satisfactions, from its vision, not its downcasting. That belief makes a difference.

During World War II, the leaders of the Allied Nations had a vision and a hope for the future. They planned to save succeeding generations from the scourge of war. On October 24, 1945 fifty-one nations signed a document and established an international organization to be known as the United Nations. The nations planned to uphold the peace. Peace on earth had to become a reality, and they were organizing to prevent the rise of another Hitler and ensure the peace. But peace is not only the absence of war. The Preamble of the Charter of the United Nations set the framework of how nations could live together and so have peace. One of the pillars of that framework states that the peoples of the UN determined to "promote social progress and better standards of life in larger freedom." That belief makes a difference.

It was during the later years of the League of Nations that the economic ans social welfare of peoples and nations came into focus as a cornerstone for peace. In the new world organization the Economic and Social Council was part of the structure of the UN established to deal specifically with the economic and social development of nations and peoples in the world.

Food: The Community-Commodity Grab Bag

"PEACE IS A WORLD WHERE BASIC HUMAN NEEDS ARE MET...AND HUMAN AND MATERIAL RESOURCES ARE SHARED FOR THE BENEFIT OF ALL PEOPLE." But this is a complicated task to fulfill, especially when a nation pits one basic need against the material resource of another nation, leaving any nation possessing neither the ability to fill a basic need nor the ability to bargain with a material resource at the mercy of the power-play groups. All of our needs are interrelated and must be met by an interrelated effort. As Mexico's President Echeverria Alvarez said at the Rome Food Conference: "What we have expounded at all international forums has been the necessity for critical awareness of the breakdown of a civilization that is attempting to uphold the thesis that the evils it suffers are autonomous and are capable of being separated one from the other, and not, as they really are, integrated and homologous forms of a world crisis within the system as a whole."[28]

Or in the words of Canada's Prime Minister Trudeau, addressing the 1975 Conference on Security and Co-operation in Europe in Helsinki: "Whatever stability this conference anticipates in Europe will be short-lived if we do not seize the opportunity now offered to us to create elsewhere the conditions necessary to permit standards of living to be raised...to provide hope for a better future for hundreds of millions of people outside Europe now existing at the subsistence level...."[29]

Food is one of the most basic human needs. In Burma the greeting is still: "Have you eaten?" For Egyptians, bread is called *aish* which means "life." Food is like atomic power. It can be used for peaceful purposes or it can be used as a weapon. When used in the latter manner, it works against peace. A lack of adequate food reserves makes a nation more insecure than a lack of guns. Insecure nations are easily frightened into actions that offset the peace of the world. This gives food an international input to a degree hardly understood in North America, where it has always existed in abundance and where the distribution of its surpluses has contributed further to the instability between nations.

The food crisis is inextricably linked to population, the environment and energy as well as to economic issues and political powers. As someone said: "The Arabs have crude, but the Americans have food." With this enormously powerful weapon in its hands the U.S. can help construct or destroy the world's delicate system of international bargaining.

Scarcity of food also means a price rise. Nearly all people in the developing nations spend between 60 to 80 percent of their income on food, whereas the figure drops to 40 percent in the eastern socialist countries and 30 percent in Britain. And the U.S. only 18 percent of personal income is needed to provide a diet including far more calories, protein and other nutrients than are in the diet of people in the developing nations. As food becomes more scarce and more expensive, famine spreads to areas normally not associated with food shortages. Food aid programs which for many years have helped alleviate famine conditions are being drastically reduced just when the need has increased. Hunger is demoralizing. Malnutrition becomes a vicious circle, something like this:

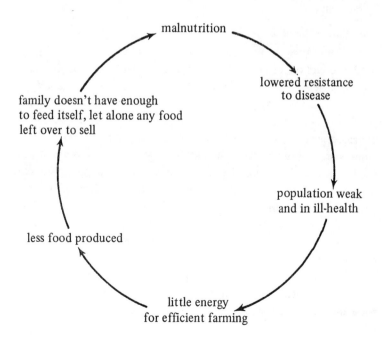

Most common deficiency diseases are due especially to the lack of sufficient protein. Protein, which supply the amino acids needed for growth and replacement of body tissues, are needed by everyone and are especially important to young children and pregnant women. The period of fastest growth for a human being is from five months before birth to ten months after birth, when the brain has reached two-thirds of its adult weight. Severe malnutrition and particularly the shortage of protein in this early period will permanently reduce the number of brain cells. This damage is irreparable and no amount of proper feeding in later years will help. It has been estimated that seven out of every ten children in the entire world are affected by protein deficiency which diminishes learning potential.

The food situation took on crisis dimension in 1972, when global production declined for the first time in 20 years. Wheat stocks of exporting countries fell to half the amount available in one year. Food reserves globally fell from a supply of 95 days in 1961 to 26 days in 1974. In the same period, the world's population increased by one-half.

The Climate Variable

There were many causes, all complex and interrelated, for the food production decline. Climatic changes were one of the main causes. Scientists say the monsoon belt around the world has shifted, resulting in severe drought in large areas such as the Sahelian region in Africa. Other areas in the world have been flooded out. Population increased at a rate of two percent a year, something like 200,000 new mouths to feed every day. With this growth, food production will need to be doubled within the next generation to maintain the present per capita consumption. But the consumption patterns of the rich nations are quite defferent from those of the poor. The average person in North America consumes nearly 2,000 pounds of grain yearly, 1,800 pounds indirectly in meat, milk, cheese and eggs. The average Indian or African consumes about 400 pounds of grain annually and all but 40 pounds directly. Growing affluence around the world has increased the demand for better and higher protein foods. Japanese per capita meat consumption rose by almost 50 percent between 1969 and 1972.

The Agri Variable

Nearly all the poor nations are in the tropical areas of the world. Agricultural technology as developed in Europe and North America is not easily adapted to the tropics. The soil is often not the same, and the rainfall distribution is different. Governments of the developing nations have tended to give low priority to agricultural devleopment, in spite of the fact that their real need was for more food. It was far easier for governments to turn to industries to strengthen the Gross National Product and thus the buying power of their nations. It is estimated that about 450 million people in the world are permanently hungry. The poor nations must grow more food themselves. Growing more food from the same amount of land means new kinds of seeds, availability of fertilizers, pesticides, new technology, efficient irrigation systems and new tools. All this means new financial investments. New seeds of the high-yielding varieties of wheat, rice and corn have been a boon to farmers. These new seeds, however, need more fertilizers and water. Petroleum-based fertilizers were the answer.

The Energy Variable

The energy crisis has further ccmplicated the food crisis . Petroleum-based fertilizers were already on the decrease when the food crisis increased the need. The increased oil prices led to the doubling or trebling of fertilizer prices in 1974. The export embargo by Japanese and U.S. fertilizer manufacturers during the 1974 crop year made matters worse. As James Grant wrote in the *New York Times*: "We are caught in an absurd cycle in which a country is refused fertilizer, thus cutting its food production and raising its import needs (and quite likely famine relief needs) by more food than the amount we produced with the withheld fertilizer in the first place, thereby further inflating already high world grain prices. This will hurt rich and poor alike." Because of the energy crisis there was no fuel for the pumps for irrigation. Farmers who had mechanized were, paradoxically, without power.

The Population Variable

The increasing population and the bleak food situation spurred the UN to call for two international conferences, the World Population Conference in Bucharest, August 1974, and the World Food Conference in Rome, November 1974.

Population policies and goals cannot be achieved without accompanying economic and social development. A farmer will continue to have a large family for economic and social reasons. In many developing nations children are the "social security" for their parents in old age. A large family increases the likelihood that at least two sons will become adults to provide this security. Moreover, a farmer needs many hands to help him. Without the means of hiring help to work in the field, he relies on family help. Children are an asset and not a liability. But certainly no parent wants to see a child starve.

Many parents would have fewer children if their lot was better.

The World Food Conference, the first political food conference, called for a World Food Council to coordinate policies concerning food production, food security and food aid. Plans to strengthen rural and agricultural development programs and many other resolutions, were among the measures adopted. What happens to implement all these goals adopted at both of these conferences will depend largely on whether nations can muster the necessary political will.

Delegates to the World Food Conference also passed a Draft Declaration on the Eradication of Hunger and Malnutrition, stating that it is the right of "every man, woman and child. . .to be free from hunger and malnutrition" and the "fundamental responsibility of the governments to work together for higher food production and more equitable and efficient distribution of food between countries and within countries." This declaration supports the definition of peace as stated in the Preface. But should governments work together for a more equitable and efficient distribution of food between countries and within countries? Can this be done? Should the nations with food help those without? To a certain degree, say some advocates of "triage" and "lifeboat ethics" theories. The proposition sounds like common sense.

Triage was a term used by the French medical corps during World War I, as a system for handling battle casualties. The wounded were divided into three groups—those who would likely live to fight again without medical help, those who would not recover even with medical aid, and those for whom medical aid would make a difference. Using this system with the nations of the world today, would nations such as India and Bangladesh and some of the countries in the African Sahel be classified as hopeless cases? Just a few miles outside Delhi, India, a large group of Indian protestors filled the highway as they marched toward the capital. Some of the banners read: "We are not ready to die yet." On being asked what they meant, a schoolteacher replied that they had read about triage.

Biologist Garret Hardin used the metaphor of the lifeboat to expound the issue further. "Metaphorically," he says, "each rich nation amounts to a lifeboat full of comparatively rich people.[30] The poor of the world are in other, much more crowded lifeboats. Continuously, so to speak, the poor fall out of their lifeboats, and swim for awhile in the water outside, hoping to be admitted to a rich lifeboat, or in some other way to benefit from the 'goodies' on board. What should the passengers on the rich lifeboat do? This is the central problem of the ethics of a lifeboat." If a helping hand is given and the drowning person is taken into the lifeboat, "the boat is swamped," says the professor, "and everyone drowns. Complete justice, complete catastrophe."

There is, however, a flaw in such logic—even in the lifeboat analogy. The waves caused by too many people struggling in the water were not taken into consideration. Too many big waves could capsize even the most luxurious lifeboat!

These seemingly plausible alternatives should be taken seriously. Who is to be fed in a food crisis must have a pragmatic solution. The lifeboat theory would be valid if the situation was such that the food for all people was not adequate. But it is a bit difficult when one-sixth of the world's population consumes almost 50 percent of the world's resources. The rich nations tell the poor nations that they must reduce their population growth because the world's resources are finite. The poor in turn point the finger at the rich and say one of your children eats more than five of ours.

The U.S. for a number of years has been sharing its surplus grain in a program called "Food for Peace." Legislative provision for this is set forth in Public Law 480. However, the food was not always sent to the neediest, and often not in correct proportion to the needs. Since 1973 such surpluses of food have diminished sharply, so the sharing becomes more critical as it is a sharing of a limited amount. Is this charity, then, or not? The question of justice comes into the picture. Is it the moral responsibility of the "haves" to share with the "have nots"? "To him who knoweth to do good and doeth it not, it is sin." If the right to eat is considered a basic human right owed to each person, and if that right is denied when the means are available to fulfil it, then there is something radically wrong with the perception of social justice. It is time the systems and mechanisms of equitable distribution in our interdependent world are revised, even restructured. But what is one's response to the National Security Council of the United States which now has final control over U.S. food surpluses and which at a recent meeting stated that, "to give food aid to countries just because people are starving is a pretty weak reason"?[31] Think of the significance of placing power over food in the National Security Council! Surely these government powers see food as a most important element in the presence or absence of peace.

11. Sharing Basic Material Resources

"PEACE IS A WORLD WHERE HUMAN AND MATERIAL (NATURAL) RESOURCES ARE SHARED FOR THE BENEFIT OF ALL PEOPLE."

The Euphrates River Debate

But in early April 1975, the crops withered along the banks of the Euphrates River in Iraq.[32] The river had not been that low the previous year. Thousands of Iraqi farmers live along the river which passes the ruins of Babylon. The low water level and the empty irrigation ditches posed a crucial problem for three million Iraqis, and the Iraqi Government blamed neighboring Syria, which had built the huge Taqba Dam across the Euphrates.

For 5,000 years the Euphrates has been used by farmers in this area; ancient canals provided water for the Hanging Gardens of Babylon, one of the seven wonders of the world. The farmers in this area were, before the overthrow of the monarchy in 1958, a group of landless peasants and small farmers. Now with the collapse of big landlords, a farm cooperative with 2,000 members was established. Among the palm trees, they planted apple trees, grapes and barley. And in little plots divided by irrigation ditches they sowed tomato, peppers, eggplants and other crops.

The Euphrates, originating in Turkey, is shared by Turkey, Syria and Iraq, then empties itself in the Persian Gulf. Both Turkey and

Syria have built large dams to generate electricity, as well as to store water for irrigation. An agreement was reached in 1974 between Iraq and the two upstream nations to allow adequate water for Iraqian agriculture after the waters behind the dams had built up to a level necessary to assure power generation. Now Iraq accused Syria of violating the agreement by denying its water rights. It has always been difficult to separate economics from politics. Iraqi officials believed that Syria's actions were politically motivated.

Iraq has always moved oil from the northern oil fields at Kirkuk to the Mediterranean via a pipeline through the Syrian port of Banias, to a refinery in Tripoli, Lebanon. This pipeline earned Syria more than $50 million a year in transit fees. Now Iraq plans to build a new pipeline to the Turkish Mediterranean coast. Syria is displeased. Syria rejected an Iraqi request for an urgent meeting of Arab foreign ministers of the Arab League on the grounds that the Euphrates problem was a technical question and did not require a meeting of Arab foreign ministers.

Is it any more moral to starve a nation out, by limiting water supply, rather than engage in an outright hot war?

The Failure of the "Trickle Down Theory"

The success of the Marshall Plan in the rebuilding of Europe after World War II was an encouragement to help the poor nations. It was presumed that if governments could raise their gross national product (GNP) the benefits would somehow trickle down. The Cold War had broken out in the 1950's, and new nations struggled to establish themselves as sovereign nations straddling the fence between the two superpowers, the U.S. and the U.S.S.R. The superpowers vied with each other in help given to the poor nations. As the superpowers rushed to industrialize and build factories, airports and dams, the governments of the poor nations envisioned a better life for their people.

In 1962 U.S. President John F. Kennedy called upon the nations of the world at the UN to engage in a development decade. The goal was to raise the GNP by 5 percent per year. It was assumed that if the total GNP of a nation was increased, the benefits would accrue to all the citizens of the nation. This is sometimes known as the "trickle

down theory." Before the end of the 1960's it was noted that although the GNP had increased in some nations, people at the bottom were gaining next to nothing. The trickle down theory was not working. In some cases the poor in the developing countries were made even poorer. The concept of development underwent revision and debate. The crucial question of the "good life" found many answers.

Indira Gandhi, Prime Minister of India, said: "The quality of life of an individual lies not in what he has but what he is. It can be measured only in his capacity to achieve harmony and resonance with his fellow human beings and with nature, to perceive the meaning of thought, and to experience the beauty of action—in short, to find joy in life. This is what will lead human beings to richer, more creative and fulfilling lives. Can this vision be achieved? The purpose of life is to believe, to hope and to strive."[33]

Our Lord, Jesus Christ said: "I came that they may have life and have it abundantly." But why did Jesus really come? We have one of the key answers to that question in John 3:16: ". . .because God so loved the world," a world he created for all the people. The present world is lopsided—overabundant on one side, with poverty and scarcity on the other. What then is the life abundant for the poor? Is it just and right that the wealth and abundance are in the hands of a few? Where is the justice?

Looking at the economic and social conditions of the world, the nations see the need for a new international economic order. In recent years world trade in manufactured goods has risen twice as fast as trade in raw materials (excluding oil). World trade is based on bargaining power. It depends on what is offered or threatened. Until recently the poor world has had very little to say about its resources. The decisions concerning prices and amounts were made by the rich and powerful nations.

Today, the interdependence of nations calls for a new approach to international relationships. Scientists now are raising the question of the amount of resources available. Is the world's wealth like a pie —only so much to go around—or is it growing? This is the important question in the economic and social development of the poor nations. How much new technology, capital investment and industry can be

94

used without catastrophic results to the world? Where are the natural resources of the world? Many of them are required by industrialized nations in order to continue to improve the present levels of life. Most of these resources are found in the developing poor nations.

The recent oil crisis, which gave a tremendous power to the oil rich nations, gave hope to other nations. Four of these nations control more than 80 percent of the world's copper exports, another four control half of the world's bauxite, the raw material for aluminum. There are other commodities such as coffee, cocoa, tin and chrome which the rich world needs and the poor, if united, could control. With this new bargaining power, the poor nations have asked for major changes in the present economic structure.

At a special session of the General Assembly of the UN in spring, 1974, the poor nations called for a new international economic order. At the regular General Assembly session in the fall of 1974, a Charter of the Economic Rights and Duties of States was adopted. This document is really a proposal for a world of cooperation. The Charter provides a vehicle to establish cooperation between the big industrial countries and the nonindustrialized ones. The Charter recognizes every nation's sovereignty over its natural resources and economic activities. There was not universal agreement on all elements of the Charter, but it will serve as a guiding policy for a number of nations in their economic thinking. One of the most controversial elements was the article dealing with transnational corporations.

Transnational Corporate Colonialism

A major phenomenon of this century has been the rapid growth of large transnational corporations that owe no allegiance to any entity except themselves. Today, more and more companies are moving across the earth setting up factories, arranging distribution outlets, looking for natural resources. These companies, established in developing countries, certainly have helped the economy of these countries. The poor have found jobs, another basic human need. The goods manufactured have provided the struggling governments with some foreign exchange. The corporations have benefited, also; labor was cheap and trade unions nonexistent. The profits have been good.

With lower costs of production the western consumer could buy

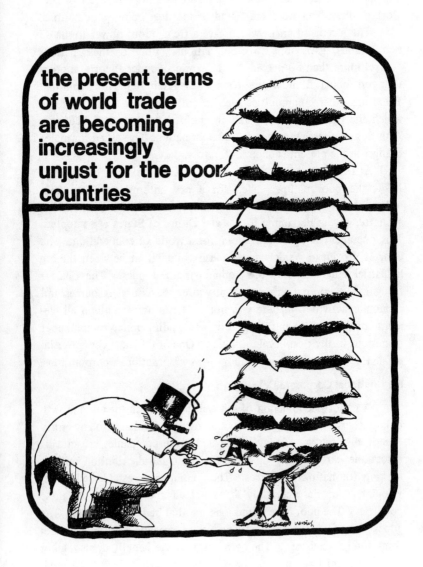

a much cheaper television set or radio than one produced in the country's headquarters nation. Here was a great possibility of combining profits with the solution to the world development problem. The aim of governments of developing countries is to increase the living levels of all their people. The aim of the corporations in these countries is to achieve higher returns for their shareholders. Can these two different goals be achieved in the same operation?

Corporations expand overseas primarily for the cheap labor. The gap between the rich and poor nations is growing. Also growing is the gap between the wages paid the union-protected worker in the West and the worker in the disorganized labor markets in developing markets. In order to produce at lowest possible cost and still make a better profit, corporations move to areas where wages are the lowest.

The transnationals form a perfect transition from the former economic colonial system. Since World War II many former colonies of western powers have become independent, sovereign states responsible for their own destinies. These nations—sometimes referred to as the "Third World," sometimes as developing nations and sometimes as less developed countries (LDCs)—are those found mainly in the tropical areas of the world, Africa, Asia and Latin America. These countries are suppliers mainly of cheap raw materials like rubber, tin, copper, jute and cotton for the industrial machinery of the western hemisphere. An economic and trade system evolved during the colonial period. Even though colonialism has ended, the system still prevails. It is a system in which the rich still make all the rules. The leaders of the developing countries would like to see the system changed. These are the poor countries often unable to provide their people enough food, water, shelter or health care, let alone jobs.

In 1954, the Japanese Company, SONY, took out a license for the transistor from Western Electric. By 1955, SONY was producing the first transistor radio using cheap labor and gearing the product specifically to the U.S. market by featuring high-quality compact radios. SONY took over the market. The cost of making transistors was reduced through advanced technology from 11 dollars in 1960 to 12 cents by 1969.

In order to stay in business U.S. electronic firms moved their factories to where labor was cheap. Giant corporations like IBM, RCA, Zenith and Philips of Holland have assembly plants in Taiwan, South Korea and Hong Kong. The result is that over 90 percent of all U.S. radios are imported.

This introduces one of the complexities of international economics as it relates to the peace or the discontent between nations. It has been said that jobs for poorer nations mean a loss of jobs for workers in the industrialized nations. American trade unionists have calculated that nearly half a million jobs were lost in the U.S. between 1965 and 1970 due to overseas based products being imported. The poor illiterate young woman or girl in any of these developing countries can assemble complex radio and television components as well as a high school graduate in Chicago. Those let go by a location change in the factory are by and large the minorities: blacks, chicanos, the women or the young. Ironically, the poor nations are thrown into competition with the most deprived sections of western society. The other side of the complexity is: would as many transistor radios, or cameras or whatever, have been sold if manufactured at higher cost in the western nations?

Governments of developing countries often tempt transnational corporations by offering various advantages, such as "tax-free holidays." Under this system there are no taxes on all foreign company profits made for the first five to ten years. Other facilities such as electrical supply, fresh water, communications and sewage disposals —all essentials to operate a foreign factory—are concentrated in the area at the host government's expense. Some governments have even provided supermarkets, lavish housing, golf courses and tennis courts for expatriate managers. But the real question is: does the developing country really benefit from the transnational corporations?

Corporations help with the large unemployment of the poor nations. The wages paid to laborers increase the currency circulation in the country. The taxes paid to the government by the company will help the economy of the country. But the wages paid to those lucky laborers do not always help the country's economy. In Mexico, over $35 million is added to the economy through the wages, rents and taxes paid by U.S. companies. But studies have shown that 65 percent of this is spent on U.S. goods or actually in the U.S. by across the border visitors. Moreover, the majority of the people, whether working in these factories or not, cannot afford to buy the goods made in their country. When some people can buy luxury goods and others who want them cannot afford them, tensions develop.

The wages paid laborers in the factories are by and large higher than the income of the peasant farmer in the neighborhood. The factory laborer gains a certain sophistication working in a western established company. With the means to try some of the "good life" western ideas he scorns the slow and traditional life-style of the farmers. The lure of the factory worker has caused more problems. Far from solving the unemployment problem, these factories can actually increase the number of jobless people. Factories are usually located in or near large towns and cities, and young people leave the countryside, refusing to work the land. For every job created in town, three people will leave the countryside, creating more social problems.

The income tax from the foreign company, after the tax-free holiday is over, is not always what it should be. Some companies close up, and move to another cheap labor location as soon as the tax shelter is removed. One of the most important threats to peace arising from transnational corporations is their potential to interfere in the internal politics of a nation. This at times involves the military might of the headquarter nation of the corporation.

The natural defense against the transnational company which is taking unfair advantage of the country's resources is to nationalize the industry or share in the development of the investment. Nationalization of foreign companies often turns political, with the governments of the headquarters of transnational corporations becoming involved.

So many times the effort to solve the economic problems of the developing country becomes similar to the story of the camel putting his head in the tent. The effort to provide a higher level of living for the people of a nation results in that which produces tension and not peace. But when the resources of a nation are threatened, and when the jobs of the prosperous are threatened, the situation does not augur well. Peace is more than the absence of war.

Carpetbag Tourism

Another area that involves big business is tourism. The dramatic increase in the level of living in most industrialized countries over the past twenty years has meant that an increased amount of discretionary income is available to spend on travel and holidays. And one of the quick resources of income for the developing countries is tourism. Tourists bring with them hard currency. Tourism also brings employment and the income helps to economy. There are, however, a few dilemmas, and many developing countries are now having second sidiary of Trans World Airlines, and the profits largely return to the parent company rather than staying in the developing country.

Foreign visitors, who delight in seeing the "quaint natives" the money spent will pay for hotel bills. Most hotels are owned and managed by western companies. Many airlines wihch provide package tours include hotel accommodations. Hilton International is a subsidary of Trans World Airlines, and the profits largely return to the parent company rather than staying in the developing country.

Foreign visitors, who delight in seeing the "quaint natives" and tour their villages, still like all the comforts in the hotels—a home away from home. Tourists spend a portion of their money on goods such as liquors, cameras and films which in most cases have to be imported. All this means that a large percentage of the income from tourism intended for the use in developing countries returns to the developed countries; sometimes as much as 40 percent as in the case of Jamaica.

While tourism provides jobs for some of the people in the country, they are more often for marginal workers. Managerial positions are usually held by expatriates. The jobs are seasonal, requiring the workers to spend some time in an air-conditioned hotel built on western standards, and sometimes in their own natural habitat. This Yo-Yo existence often produces tensions. The "good life" of the foreigner, imitated by the local elite, leaves the marginal worker with a sense of frustration and a dislocation of traditional values.

The economic war continues. The battle lines are not clear, making it all the more difficult to see how the situation militates against peace. Frustration with the unrealized hard money gain; frustration and confused expectations among the participants; misunderstanding on the part of the tourists—all contribute to friction and not peace.

12. Tomorrow Made Possible

For the past few years, with the focus on the enviroment, we have become more and more conscious of our global world. *Only One Earth*, a book by Barbara Ward and Rene Dubos, means just that. This global consciousness, a one-world concept, created an awareness of "interdependence"—a word now in vogue. The oil embargo in the fall of 1973 struck home more forcibly our interdependence. Interdependence projects a feeling of neighborliness, a kind of selfless brotherhood. Interdependence makes every crisis in every part of the world the business of everybody. Are there dangers in this concept? Will our interdependence complicate world crises to a dangerous level?

Oil Peddlers

The oil crisis made the world aware that the reserves of oil and gas are fast running out. Even the oil producing countries which had formed the Organization of Petroleum Exporting Countries (OPEC) believe that conservation of oil reserves is essential to prevent a catastrophe. If consumption remains at the 1973 level, the known reserves of oil and gas would be exhausted in 40 years.

Warnings such as this have been given over a period of years, but it wasn't until the Arab embargo that most nations began to realize that there may come a time, quite soon, when there will not be any oil available at any price. OPEC members are thinking in terms of reducing production so that the reserves could last more than 40 years. This, of course, would affect the life-style of many western nations. It would affect the developing nations as well, even though nearly all oil imported into the poorest nations is used for essentials such as public transport and generation of electricity.

Effective energy-productin substitutes for oil are being researched. However, the investment will be staggering. Cost of exploiting deep mined coal in the U.S. is six times more expensive than Arab oil; oil shale and coal gas twenty-five times more expensive. Many countries are looking for less expensive substitutes. Geothermal power can generate electricity. Solar energy and the power of ocean waves are still in the experimental stage. Nuclear power is considered a safer and cleaner alternative way of providing the power needed.

It must remain in the center of attention that it is economic pressure which is to be considered here. A poorer nation wants to develop its resources or provide opportunity for new industry. To do this requires energy. Nuclear energy has proved to be a fair competitor to fossil fuels, especially when the nations with the components for nuclear energy are willing to use them under the guise of international aid to ensure friendship plus a market for sophisticated machinery. Having played the games with the dangerous marbles provides the real opportunity for alternate uses. A knife can be used to kill or to cure. Energy-poor nations have little hope of meeting needs of people.

Uranium/Plutonium Peddlers

Today, there are 131 nuclear power reactors producing 45 billion watts of electricity in eighteen countries. By 1980 there may be fifteen times more reactors. Enriched uranium will be needed to fuel atomic plants.

There is no absolute way to prevent the use of these materials for military purposes. An enriched uranium plant can give a country the capability of producing weapons—grade uranium, the material normally used to trigger an H-bomb. Moreover, a by-product of nuclear power reaction is plutonium. There are also breeder reactors that will completely replace the present burner type reactors. The breeder reactors are fueled by plutonium. Plutonium is suitable for immediate use in nuclear weapons. There are already fifty countries operating plutonium producing reactors or research reactors. These reactors are producing thousands of kilograms of plutonium each year.

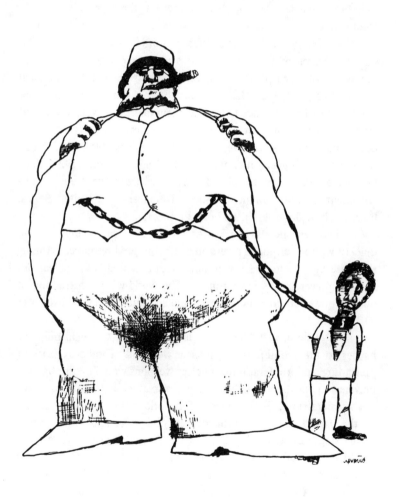

Just 10 kilograms of plutonium is more than enough to produce one nuclear weapon. The dangerous situation cannot be minimized. Plutonium is extremely toxic and costly. Such material in the hands of a terrorist could be trouble for the world. Safeguards are needed not only within the states which have reactors. Credible political and technology barriers are needed to prevent the possibilities of "a bomb-a-week."

The Treaty on the Nonproliferation of Nuclear Weapons (NPT), signed in March of 1970, stated that non-nuclear states, party to the Treaty, would accept safeguards as prepared by the International Atomic Energy Agency (IAEA). But the treaty is not a completely effective instrument, since two of the main nuclear powers, China and France, and a number of potential nuclear powers like Israel, India, Brazil and South Africa have not associated themselves with it. Japan and Egypt have signed, but not ratified it. One of the main obligations under the Treaty was to take effective measures toward nuclear disarmament. Even Britain, the Soviet Union and the United States, however, have done very little in that respect.

There are nearly ten nations capable of producing a bomb quickly without crippling diversion of their natural resources. Among them are Egypt and Israel, who have both accepted U.S. nuclear aid. Nuclear power means big business. The world-wide construction of nuclear power stations alone represents an annual investment of over $10 billion.

As fragile as it is, the Treaty is at this point the main political barrier to the proliferation of nuclear weapons. The best chance of preventing the proliferation of nuclear weapons would be through the universal application of IAEA safeguards to all peaceful nuclear activities within a state. It is a tragedy for world security that the parties to the Treaty have not fulfilled their obligation under the Treaty. Some steps, even small ones, taken toward nuclear disarmament would have greatly reinforced the Treaty. Because the main nuclear power states have not done this, and because of that, do not solidly back the Treaty, the world is faced with the emergence of many more nuclear weapon powers. The survival of the world will be even more threatened in the future than it is today.

Arms Peddling

This is a lopsided world. The "have nots" outnumber the "haves," and the division of the world resources is unbalanced. Even in this imbalance, there is the problem of priorities. This is not the place to discuss the use of weaponry for "defense," or what is more realistic for maintaining balance of power. But how does the expenditure for military hardware affect the internal economic situation of a nation? The Gross National Product for the world in 1972 was estimated at \$4,0555,174 million. Out of this amount \$221,680 million was spent on the military and \$57,817 million for international peace keeping. This means that while hundreds of millions of people in the world lack the basic necessities of life, the governments of the world spend \$221 million on the necessities of death.

If only a few hundred nuclear bombs at most will virtually destroy civilization, what is the need for a stockpiling of thousands—over 7,000 already for the strike? It has been estimated that there is now an "overkill" thirty to forty times for every human being on this earth. One can be dead, but hardly worth all that expense to be deader!

The answer is both political and economic. Defense is big business. The U.S. has had a military based economy for the past 30 years. One of the factors in the emergence from the Depression of the Thirties was the advent of Adolph Hitler. Churchhill made a plea to the U.S.: "We have the men, give us the tools." The economic machinery of the U.S. was willing to turn out the tools of war. Part of the problem is that the nation has never really retooled since. Not all the responsibility for the lethargy in retooling is on the warmongers. Many connumities rely for a large portion of their jobs and industrial health on government contracts. When conversion to peacetime production is proposed, the new needs might be met in another community and jobs are lost, politicans place pressure, and then. . .

Millions of people work in the various factories producing weaponry. Hence about \$25 billion is spent a year for military research and development, while \$4 billion is the yearly expenditure for all medical research.

The chart below taken from "World Military and Social Expenditures 1974" by Ruth Leger Sivard, states: "Comparisons of the military and social ranking of countries indicate that for most of the biggest military powers armed strength has been achieved at the sacrifice of the social welfare. With few exceptions, major powers stand lower in the ranking of nations in social indicators than in military."

The arms trade is a most prosperous business today. Recently the trade has been brisk with the buying power of the oil-rich nations. In February 1975, Egypt spent more than $900 million, buying from the West and from the U.S.S.R. Five other developing countries helped to swell the amount to more than $2.2 billion, Ethopia and Pakistan spending $50 million each while Spain and Kuwait spent $200 and $350 million respectively. Iran bought $700 million worth of arms. Last year the international sales of arms and ammunition exceeded $20 billion.

The biggest arms peddler in the world is the U.S. Since 1960 the U.S. has sold an estimated $90 billion worth of death machinery abroad, a sum far greater than all the foreign aid extended by it to the poor nations. In 1974, the U.S. captured 46 percent of the world total arms sale. The U.S.S.R. is the second biggest seller, selling 400 supersonic planes in 1974, compared to the 350 exported by the U.S. Italy, Britain, France, West Germany, Switzerland, Sweden and Canada are some of the major producers and peddlers of arms.

The major buyers, unfortunately, are the less developed countries. A show of military strength is important to the prestige of developing countries. Often the hardware is bought not for defense purposes but to control the riots and revolutions of the poor people. In other cases the border clashes between two countries are fought out with weapons purchased from the same western nation.

The irony of the arms sales has focused attention on the Middle East. The oil embargo and the tremendous rise in price for oil added billions of dollars to the revenues of the Arab nations. What better way to spend the money than to purchase weapons.

With the purchase of modern weaponry, the need for special training in the use of such was needed. In the spring of 1974 it was

MAJOR MILITARY POWERS*
AND THEIR RANK IN SOCIAL INDICATORS, 1972

Country	Military Expenditures $US Million	Military Expenditures Rank	Education Public Expenditures Per Capita	Education School-age Population Per Teacher	Education Illiteracy	Health Care Public Expenditures Per Capita	Health Care Population Per Physician	Health Care Infant Mortality Per 1000	International Peacekeeping Public Expenditures Per Capita	Foreign Economic Aid Public Expenditures Per Capita
United States	77,638	1	4	12	1	5	17	13	5	12
USSR	65,000	2	14	36	1	16	2	25	42	20
Germany, West	9,018	3	10	23	1	2	10	24	19	14
China	9,000	4	88	51	22	97	89	80	—	25
United Kingdom	8,186	5	15	9	19	12	26	13	8	16
France	7,286	6	18	12	1	8	23	9	23	4
Italy	3,675	7	23	12	26	33	9	31	20	20
Japan	2,628	8	21	20	1	54	30	4	27	15
Canada	2,258	9	2	6	25	4	15	13	4	3
India	2,112	10	109	64	83	97	78	93	56	—
Poland	1,945	11	28	35	21	21	14	31	56	—
Germany, East	1,906	12	22	17	13	17	11	13	—	—
Iran	1,637	13	64	92	81	57	68	102	42	—
Netherlands	1,552	14	5	38	1	6	25	1	7	6
Czechoslovakia	1,543	15	23	28	13	10	4	23	42	—
Spain	1,515	16	42	41	24	47	23	33	56	25
Israel	1,490	17	19	9	40	32	1	20	32	23
Sweden	1,451	18	1	3	1	1	22	1	1	5
Australia	1,411	19	13	9	29	19	32	11	10	9
Brazil	1,256	20	63	31	61	86	51	76	25	—
Egypt	1,136	22	73	91	90	67	48	85	38	—
Belgium	1,015	21	8	1	13	11	13	20	14	8

*All countries with military expenditures above $1 billion in 1972

**From Table III, pp. 22-27. The rank order number is repeated if more than one country has the same figure.

Copyright by Ruth Sivard. Published by Ruth Sivard. Used by permission. Charts and projections are from Ruth Sivard, World Military and Social Expenditures, 1974. (WMSE Publications, Box 1003, Leesburg, Va. 20075; $2.00 per copy.)

disclosed that the Pentagon had hired a U.S. company to train Saudi Arabia's 26,000 man national guard. This company began recruiting 1,000 former U.S. military veterans for the three-year- job.

The irony is that it was Saudi Arabia who first proposed the oil embargo on the U.S. during one of the Middle East crises. The Arab countries hinted that if the Middle East situation was not settled soon another boycott was possible. The disruptions caused all over the world by the 1973 embargo would be even worse with the next embargo. Secretary of State Kissinger, involved with the complicated task of settling the Middle East issue with his "shuttle diplomacy," declared that if a new oil embargo threatened the strangulation of the industrial world, an armed invasion to seize the oil wells would be a solution.

A cartoon in the *Los Angeles Times* clearly states the dilemma. Together with a picture of a figure in Arabian dress with the pointed finger are the words: "Uncle Sam Wants You (to train Saudi Arabian National Guard Troops to Protect Oil Fields Against the United States). Enlist Now."[34] The fact is that the regular forces of Saudi Arabia and Iran already have been trained by the U.S. military. The deal with Saudi Arabia was a $335 million enterprise. Many of the components of the enterprise are handled by civilian companies. The economy is a war economy.

There was concern that the former U.S. veterans would be drawn into a war. "We are not mercenaries because we are not pulling the triggers." "We train people to pull triggers," said one officer who signed on for the job. Another officer laughed and added: "Maybe that makes us executive mercenaries."

President Dwight D. Eisenhower said in 1953: "Every gun that is made, every warship launched, every rocket fired signifies, in a final sense, a theft from those who hunger and are not fed, those who are cold and are not clothed. This world in arms is not spending money alone. It is spending the sweat of its laborers, the genius of its scientists, the hopes of its children. . . ."

It has been estimated that $1.5 billion could eliminate illiteracy over a 5-year period. With the food crisis still hovering over nations, $2 billion could provide universal family planning services while $4 billion could provide special feeding programs for the world's 200 million undernourished children. As long as nations choose to spend their money for that which is not bread, there will be hungry people. The basic human needs will not be met. There can be no peace among the peoples.

Peddling a New Life Over the Air

The earth has become a smaller and tighter planet due mainly to mass communications. News is flashed around the world even as it takes place. The remotest corner of the earth is in instant communication with the rest of the world through transistor radio. Ham radios operate all over the world. Television brings the world right into one's home. There is a deluge of printed material, almost impossible to assimulate.

The economist, Jan Tinbergen, once said:

> The size of the gap between the rich and the poor
> TIMES (X)
> The extent of awareness of the poor of the gap
> EQUALS (=)
> The degree of violence which can be anticipated.

Before World War II most of the people of developing countries, then colonies of western powers, accepted their situation as part of fate or destiny, even as their leaders struggled to gain independence. Mass communications have enlightened these people so that they no longer think that being permanently hungry is part of life. In the flush of gaining freedom as independent sovereign states it was thought there would be a better life. The "rising expectations" of poor people were understandable. Most expectations were, however, long in coming and in some areas situations had even worsened. Violence had to be put down. Then often the army who brought order took control.

Life has not changed much for the majority of the people in these areas. The little boy in the hills of Burma during World War II who played a small bamboo flute while he watched and tended the family water buffalo, is replaced by his son tending the family water buffalo. The son's music is canned, coming through his small transistor radio. Interspersed in the music he hears the message of the good life, which compounds his frustration. He is a frustrated boy who knows that if he had the opportunity he could be the pilot of the plane flying across the skies.

Life in the developed countries has improved vastly, and television with all its commercials has drawn attention to the good life available; all that one needs is a lot of money. Discontent and frustrations do not spell peace.

Kennety Boulding said: "If the human race is to survive, it will have to change its ways of thinking more in the next twenty-five years than in the last 25,000." Those twenty-five years have almost run their course. Unfortunately, thought patterns of old still exist—stereotypes and cliches still persist. Such cliches that Asians don't value life, for instance, could distort policies of other nations.

In the book *The Art of Rapid Reading* by Walter Pitkin, first published in 1929 and reprinted in 1962, there is a sentence that bears pondering: "Ignorance is safer than misinformation." A great deal of unrest, suspicion and distrust comes from misinformation. Words are mutilated or distorted. They have lost their original meanings. The jargon of today is outdated tomorrow. A few years ago "war on poverty" and "war on hunger" were the cries of action. These are words of aggression. If they really conveyed what they mean, there would have been the same kind of mobilization of energy and effort, research, money and people and all the inventiveness one finds for a military war, in order to carry on the war against poverty or hunger.

Our Future Vision

Is there hope for humanity? Is there hope to build peace? President John F. Kennedy said: "Too many of us think that peace is impossible, unreal. But that is a dangerous, defeatist belief. It leads to the conclusion that war is inevitable; that mankind is doomed; that we are gripped by forces we cannot control. Our problems are man-made. They can be solved by man."

Robert Heilbroner in his book *An Inquiry Into the Human Prospect* feels there is little hope for humanity. According to Heilbroner, population growth, environmental deterioration, the spread of nuclear weapons and the inevitable slowing down of economic growth, are changes which add up to inevitable disaster. The poor

world will become poorer, and more desperate, and its increasingly authoritarian governments will threaten "wars of redistribution" against the rich nations. In addition to this external threat, the rich countries will face irresistible pressure from internal redistribution of wealth as pollution and scarcity of raw materials dictate a drastic slowing down of economic growth. Heilbroner does not believe that the advanced capitalist or socialist nations are capable of dealing with the tensions which these two demands will create and that both will become politically more authoritarian and may wage "wars of pre-emptive seizure" against the poor world in order to secure for themselves vital raw materials. The result will be famine, environmental disaster, war and repression.

A few years ago, the Club of Rome, a group of international scientists, published a report on "Limits to Growth." It was a widely publicized, controversial report which predicted the collapse of present global structures sometime in the twenty-first century. Using computerized models the researchers studied five basic factors in the world system: population, agricultural production, natural resources, industrial production and pollution. Data related to these factors were fed into a computer along with formulas that specified possible quantitative relations among the factors. For example: if a country or area had this much population, then so much agricultural production was needed, which meant this much fertilizer and this much pesticide, resulting in so much pollution and so on. The grim results startled the world, because the massage said there were limits to what the world can do—there were limits to growth.

This report, as may well be imagined, received various responses. Some believe that a worsening of economic conditions is inevitable. Resources are being depleted. There are absolute limits to the amount of heat gained (from industry) that our planet earth can tolerate. Opponents of the report are critical of the doomsday approach. The unresearched mineral resources have not been accounted for; more food could be grown by newer methods. There are some in the developing countries who say that such reporting is the work of an imperialistic, capitalistic society bent on maintaining domination over poorer areas by stopping the growth of their industries.

Consider for a moment that one of the problems in tropical areas is the growth of water hyacinths. They are beautiful when they begin their growth. Suppose they doubled in size each day in an area that would be covered in 30 days. When would the hyacinths move from looking pretty to covering the pond? On the 29th day, of course.

While there are many who criticized the study for this straight line methodology, the collapse portrayed in the report has already characterized the problem in some parts of the developing countries. The impact of this study, published in 1972, has initiated more studies and research and conferences to respond to the questions raised. It has been translated into 26 languages. All such studies and information have made societies and nations more globally conscious. Margaret Mead wrote: "For the first time human beings throughout the world, in their information about one another and responses to one another, have become a community that is united by shared knowledge and danger."

Dennis Meadows, leader of the team who produced "Limits to Growth," in an interview conducted by Robert G. Hanvey said: "The oil crisis, mounting famine and the steady deterioration of the environment all illustrate our central thesis. We suggested that if society can deliberately initiate policies in anticipation of its limits, the result will be much more satisfactory than if nature picks a set of pressures that will stop growth. Our goal was to encourage deliberate programs that would bring equilibrium before it is forced on mankind."

The question really is: "How much is enough?"

There is a second report from the Club of Rome called: "Mankind at the Turning Point" by authors, Professor Mihajlo Mesarovic, head of the Systems Research Center of Case Western Reserve University in Ohio, and Patrick Eduard Pestel of the Technical University in Hanover, Germany. The Mesarovic-Pestel study, like the first study, involved computer analysis of huge amounts of data on resources, population and pollution; but with a strong emphasis on policy exploration. In this kind of computer analysis, the analyst puts formulas into the computer that represent his or her assumptions about the quantitative relationships between various factors. Then he or she can play with these factors. For example: if region "A" decides on population policy "X" what will happen to the food situation? If it decides on population policy "Z" what will happen?

The predictions are disturbing, especially for some regions of the world. The authors believe this is the end of an era of independence. We are on the threshold of a new era that will usher in an integrated world system. Though sober in spirit and honest in its presentation of the challenges confronting humanity, the book does not predict inevitable disaster. Instead, in a positive, hopeful spirit it presents alternative paths of action, called "scenarios," which the authors claim may save us from potential catastrophe.

In a recent interview (conducted by Robert G. Hanvey) speaking about the scenario for the food situation in South Asia, Professor Mesarovic believes "South Asia cannot possibly pay for this food . . .it must be helped to develop its own industries so that it has something to ship back. Essentially, that means a diversification of industry, a division of labor all around the world. So really the way to increase our own standard of living and help these other people is to integrate as far as industrial development is concerned."

Here come some of these dilemmas again. More industries mean more consumption of resources. And if there are limits to growth, how could this problem be resolved. Professor Mesarovic said that: "The questions really are the limits to what, at what time, and where"? He suggested that the West must allow the developing nations to use more resources in order to develop and grow, and at the same time the industrialized countries should use less for the sake of the developing countries and for their own sake.

This would require a change in attitude. The dinosaur perished because it did not know how to adapt to the changing conditions in the world centuries ago.

During the Japanese occupation of Burma, in World War II, the conquerors turned out vast quantities of paper money to buy food mainly for the armies. Inflation rose rapidly as more paper money flooded the markets. An enormous bag packed tightly with thousands of rupees was needed to buy food for one day. When the war started going badly for the Japanese, hill tribes would refuse to accept the paper money. Coins or money produced during the British era had to be used. Few people had such currency, and those who did were not anxious to spend it. Rice was at a premium. Gold was exchanged for a bag of rice. Broken rice normally fed to chickens became the medium of exchange. A small six-ounce can of broken rice bought a small cauliflower. Two such cans saw a large fish in the pot. Barter was the order of the day. It was the only alternative to starvation.

Maybe the dinosaur had an excuse, he did not know of the changes taking place, neither did he know what were some of the predictions. The world today cannot have that excuse. There is enough written, and while there is a realization of a finite globe, and a great deal of rhetoric of interdependence, this age is still one of independence, nationalism and regionalism. The reconciliation between nationalism and interdependence is a difficult one. Present-day society is global because present-day technology is. Technology has now knit together into a single society all human beings all around the globe. Can civilization survive in this single society? Whereas civilization in Victorian times meant culture and religion, civilization now means science and technology.

The irony is that this very civilization could be destroyed by the same means that can make it. According to Rene Dubos in his book *Beast or Angel*: "Civilizations are mortal, but they can be revived and transformed by human imagination, fantasy and will. . . .Crises are practically always a source of enrichment and of renewal because they encourage the search for new solutions. These solutions cannot come from a transformation of human nature, because it is not possible to change genetic endowment of the human species. But they can come from the manipulation of social structure. because these affect the quality of behavior and of the environment and therefore the quality of life." Man has the power to change.

How does one change? In step order: (1) understand the problems in one's country that affect or are affected by other peoples; (2) understand some of the greatest threats to civilization or world order, such as nuclear holocaust, economic injustices, starvation and environment, inflation; (3) get the best people in seats of power, who would then be aware of the thinking from people at all levels; (4)

understand the attitudes of others; and (5) What does justice mean in an interdependent world? Is "I am my brother's keeper" relavent? Maybe the western approach of "I am my brother's keeper," leading to an ethic of action, could be related to the eastern concept of "I *am* my brother," which projects an awareness of a common ground of being.

A few years ago, Arnold Toynbee in writing on *The Future of Mankind* and what ails human beings said: "We shall not win an alternative society without winning an alternative religion: for religion is society's rock bottom basis. Our present religion is a consecration of egoism. Our present ultimate objective is the anti-social pursuit of material gain, both individual and collective. Since this is an abominable religion, it is not surprising that we are making ourselves miserable and are jeopardizing mankind's survival."

There is nothing wrong with Christ's teaching, only the way it has been understood. Jesus said: "Seek first the kingdom and these things will be added unto you," but the religion of egoism seeks first the things and hopes the kingdom will be added.

Notes

1. John Howard Yoder, The Politics of Jesus (Grand Rapids, Mich.: Eerdmans Press, 1972). See Chapter three.
2. From an unpublished statement used as background in the preparation of the NCC Policy Statement on Hunger.
3. Robert McAfee Brown, Religion and Violence (Philadelphia: The Westminster Press, 1973).
4. Brown, Ibid.
5. Brown, Ibid.
6. Ned O'Gorman, "Desperate Plight of Black Children Born into Poverty in Harlem, New York City—Inaction and 'Vast Silence' About Situation," New York Times, section 6, p. 10, June 1, 1975.
7. Emmanuel Mounier, L'Engagement de la Foi (Paris: Seuil, 1933).
8. See Dom Helder Camara, Spiral of Violence (Denville, N.J.: Dimension Books, 1971).
9. Reprinted in Origins, N.C. Documentary Service (National Catholic News Service), February 13, 1975.
10. Gary MacEoin, "U.S. Mission Efforts Threatened by CIA 'Dirty Tricks,' " St. Anthony Messenger, March, 1975.
11. Paulo Freire, Pedagogy of the Oppressed (New York: Herder and Herder, 1971).
12. Brown, Religion and Violence.
13. Thomas Merton, Faith and Violence (Notre Dame, Indiana: University of Notre Dame Press, 1968).
14. Martin Luther King, Jr., Letter from Birmingham City Jail (Philadelphia: American Friends Service Committee, 1963).
15. Thomas Merton, ed., Gandhi on Non-Violence (New York: New Directions, 1964).
16. Merton, Faith and Violence.
17. Betty Richardson Nute, Helder Camara's Latin America (London: Friends Peace and International Relations Committee, n.d.).
18. Albert Bigelow, "Why I Am Sailing Into the Pacific Bomb-Test Area," Liberation, February, 1958.
19. Letter quoted in Denver Post, November 9, 1971.
20. "Go Up, Moses," recorded by Roberta Flack; Atlantic Recording Corporation. Composition published by Sapphire Music, New York.
21. Gene Sharp, The Politics of Non-Violent Action (Boston: Porter Sargent, 1973).

22. Jorge Lara-Braud, Social Justice and the Latin Churches (Atlanta: John Knox Press, 1969).
23. "Death of a Freedom Fighter," Critic, March-April, 1975.
24. Brian J. Hall and Maury Smith, Value Clarification as Learning Process (New York: Paulist Press, 1974).
25. Louis Rath, Merrill Harmin, Sidney R. Simon, Values and Teaching. Quoted in Hall and Smith, op. cit.
26. Ibid.
27. See Ronald E. Galbraith and Thomas M. Jones, "Teaching Strategies for Moral Dilemmas: An Application of Kohlberg's Theory of Moral Development to the Social Studies Classroom," Social Education, January, 1975.
28. Center Focus, January, 1975.
29. Canada Weekly, Vol. 3, No. 33, August 13, 1975.
30. New Internationalist, July, 1975.
31. "Use of Food to Aid U.S. Interests Hit," Washington Post, December 9, 1974.
32. Background for this section taken from The New York Times, April 13, 1975.
33. Saturday Review/World, December 14, 1974.
34. Time Magazine, February 24, 1975.